When New Wine

TRUE
REVIVAL?
OR
LAST DAYS
DECEPTION?

Makes
a Man Divine

ROGER
OAKLAND

When New Wine Makes a Man Divine
by Roger Oakland

Copyright © 1997 Understand The Times

Printed in the United States of America

ISBN: 0-9637797-5-3

Library of Congress Catalog Card #: 97–090481

Except where otherwise indicated, all Scripture quotations are taken from the King James Version of the Bible.

I marvel that ye are so soon removed from him that called you into the grace of Christ unto another gospel: Which is not another; but there be some that trouble you, and would pervert the gospel of Christ.

Galatians 1:6–7

Table of Contents

Prologue

Christianity is facing a crisis today. Many voices are promoting various messages which contradict one another. While some say we are in the midst of the greatest revival the world has ever seen, others are saying that an end-times deception is happening in the name of Christ. Are people being drawn into a counterfeit form of Christianity which may actually be preparing the way for the Antichrist, or is such a view unbiblical and unfair?

Over the past several years, as I have traveled around the world, I have been troubled by the trend I have seen unfolding in the name of Christ. Although there seems to be more and more people being attracted to Christianity, many of the ideas and teachings associated with this movement are not found in the Bible. Even though millions of people are boldly claiming they have experienced Christ in a new way by encountering some sort of sensation, feeling, emotion or physical phenomenon, the Scriptures do not mention that these are the kinds of things believers should be seeking after in preparation for the Second Coming of Jesus Christ.

New Wine or Old Deception? is the title of a book I previously authored to help believers understand the dangers of an experience-based Christianity and to exhort them back to a faith based upon the Word of God. However, since that book was published, a trend to embrace Christianity based upon experiences that stimulate the flesh has only continued to escalate. Called the New Wine movement, the behavior now being embraced and promoted in many places around the world is becoming more and more bizarre each day.

Although many are still saying, "Some of the New Wine is from God and some is not," or "We shouldn't throw away the baby with the bath water," I am convinced that the people who are saying these things are not heeding the warnings laid out in the Bible. The Bible clearly declares that a falling away from the faith inspired by the doctrines of demons will take place before Jesus Christ returns to this earth.[1]

Instead of warning people about this time of deception, a growing number of teachers and church leaders today now claim that Christians are being prepared to become part of a mighty army of God that He will use to usher in the Second Coming of Jesus. Basing their ideas on the questionable doctrines of the "Latter Rain" movement which originated in Canada in the

---

1. 1 Timothy 4:1.

1940's, these New Winers announce that Christians are being empowered by a mighty outpouring of the Holy Spirit, known as the "Third Wave."

Rather than promoting a gospel of repentance and pointing the lost to who Jesus is and what He has done, the new gospel emphasizes experiencing God. This new gospel, also called the "new thing," promotes experiences that can be measured by feelings and emotions. A personal encounter with signs, wonders, and miracles is often used as a measuring stick which determines whether or not one has arrived.

Although today many pastors are warning people to watch out for the prophetic signs which indicate the return of Jesus Christ is at hand, very seldom do we hear much about the "apostasy" that will be taking place in the church. In fact, rather than warning people about being deceived by "another gospel," an "ecumenical gospel" is being promoted which joins believers and unbelievers in the name of Christ.

The theme of this book is based on a trend which Paul suggested we should look for in the closing days of time. He said there would be a combination of events happening before Jesus returned that would unite a counterfeit gospel with a counterfeit Christ. In his own words:

> Let no man deceive you by any means: for that day shall not come, except there come a falling away first, and that man of sin be revealed, the

son of perdition; Who opposeth and exalteth himself above all that is called God, or that is worshipped; so that he as God sitteth in the temple of God, showing himself that he is God.[2]

It is my conviction that the deception Paul warned us about is taking place right now. I know that many people who profess the name of Jesus will strongly disagree. Many of the things I will be documenting and categorizing as deception, others will insist are blessings from God.

It is my desire that everyone who reads this book will be drawn to the Bible and check out all that I have written according to the Scriptures. How else can we evaluate whether something is right or wrong?

And finally, ask yourself this question: If "another gospel" is being proclaimed and people are being deceived, what should we do? It is my prayer that Christians would get back to the true gospel. Jesus said the gospel of the Kingdom would be proclaimed unto all the nations and then the end would come.[3] Let's get on with the job before it's too late.

Roger Oakland

---

2 2 Thessalonians 2:3–4.

3. Matthew 24:14.

PART I
New Wine

1
Another Gospel

The gospel of Jesus Christ is not complicated. John summarized the greatest truth in the history of the world this way—"For God so loved the world, that he gave his only begotten Son, that whosoever believeth in him should not perish, but have everlasting life."[4] Or, saying the same statement in another way: believing in who Jesus is and what He has done is the only way to heaven. So why doesn't everyone just believe and head down this road towards eternal life? The answer is simple! Satan, God's enemy, wants man to go to hell with him. According to the Bible, the majority of people in the world are following him and they don't even know it.

IT'S THE GOOD NEWS

The word *gospel* simply means "good news." This message proclaims that the God of the universe has provided a way for sinful people to

---

4. John 3:16.

become sons and daughters of God and share eternity with Him. Throughout history the gospel has transformed countless millions of lives. People who have placed their trust in Jesus Christ have recognized God's grace and received the gift of eternal life.

IT'S A NARROW WAY

Although the gospel is a simple message, there are many ways to complicate it by adding to or taking away from its truth. When Jesus was speaking to His disciples at the Sermon on the Mount, He explained that there are two widely contrasting pathways that lead to the eternal destination of mankind.[5]

The wide way, He said, is traveled by the majority of people, whose destiny will be eternal separation from God. Following Jesus is the narrow road which leads to eternal life—a road less commonly traveled.

Christianity, then, is clearly based on Jesus' own words that He is the only way.[6] However, recognizing that Satan has an agenda to deceive mankind, we should not be surprised that a part of his deceptive plan is focused on trying to get people to think they believe God's plan of salvation when they really do not.

---

5. Matthew 7:13–14.
6. John 14:6.

THERE'S ANOTHER GOSPEL

Paul's warning to the Galatians regarding their eagerness to accept "another gospel" is something all Bible-believing Christians should review from time to time. Emphasizing that the message of salvation must never be compromised, Paul wrote:

> I marvel that ye are so soon removed from him that called you into the grace of Christ unto another gospel: Which is not another; but there be some that trouble you, and would pervert the gospel of Christ. But though we, or an angel from heaven, preach any other gospel unto you than that which we have preached unto you, let him be accursed. As we said before, so say I now again, If any man preach any other gospel unto you than that ye have received, let him be accursed.[7]

It is obvious that the sentence for contaminating the gospel with false teaching is serious and should not be taken lightly. We must always be careful not to get caught in the trap the Galatians fell into. Recall the words Paul chose when he reprimanded them:

> O foolish Galatians, who hath bewitched you, that ye should not obey the truth, before whose eyes Jesus Christ hath been evidently set forth, crucified among you?[8]

---

7. Galatians 1:6–9.
8. Galatians 3:1.

Should not that same reprimand echo down through the generations to our time? Are Christians today not subject to the same kind of subtle deception that captured the Galatians? Is it possible for genuine Bible believers to accept a counterfeit gospel which is not completely centered around the finished work of the cross?

When it comes to checking out our ideas about the way we understand the gospel, we must never deviate from the Word of God. Today we live in a world where many people are making numerous claims in the name of Christianity. These are times when we need to hold fast to God's Word and defend the truth with diligence and a sound mind. If we base our eternity on experiences that are not biblically grounded, there is a strong chance we will be deceived.

2

A Counterfeit Gospel for a Counterfeit Christ

According to the Bible, the period of history that unfolds before the return of Jesus Christ will be characterized by great deception. Jesus and Paul both warned about false prophets and false teachers who would prepare the way for the false Messiah by performing signs and wonders as part of a deceptive plan. What is even more startling is the revelation given to us that this time of deception is to involve people being deceived in the name of Christ. Could we be living in this very time that was prophesied so many years ago?

DECEPTION IN HIS NAME

When it comes to the subject of what kind of spiritual deception will take place before Jesus returns, the Bible gives us clear answers. When Jesus was asked by His disciples what signs could be expected indicating His return would be soon, He replied:

> Take heed that no man deceive you. For many
> shall come in my name, saying, I am Christ;
> and shall deceive many.[9]

Then, further clarifying what to expect regarding this deception that would take place in the end times, Jesus continued:

> Then if any man shall say unto you, Lo, here is
> Christ, or there; believe it not. For there shall
> arise false Christs, and false prophets, and shall
> show great signs and wonders; insomuch that,
> if it were possible, they shall deceive the very
> elect.[10]

A FALLING AWAY

Paul the apostle also added another dimension to the warning Jesus gave regarding this time when some would claim to be God. In 2 Thessalonians he stated that a counterfeit Messiah would arise one day and perform many false signs and wonders. Before this counterfeit Messiah would appear there would be a period characterized by a time of apostasy—a falling away from the faith—a time when even Bible-believing Christians would be deceived. He stated:

> Let no man deceive you by any means: for that
> day shall not come, except there come a falling
> away first, and that man of sin be revealed, the
> son of perdition; Who opposeth and exalteth

---

9. Matthew 24:4–5.
10. Matthew 24:23–24.

himself above all that is called God, or that is worshipped; so that he as God sitteth in the temple of God, showing himself that he is God.[11]

Then, making it clear where this self-proclaimed god-man will receive his power to deceive his followers, Paul continued:

Even him, whose coming is after the working of Satan with all power and signs and lying wonders, And with all deceivableness of unrighteousness in them that perish; because they received not the love of the truth, that they might be saved.[12]

Today, in certain evangelical circles, the word *apostasy* has been censored from the vocabulary of many pastors speaking from the pulpit. This "falling away from the faith" has already occurred, some have said. The age we live in is a time of refreshment or renewal. Now is a time when God is pouring His Spirit upon the world and people are experiencing His "anointing" in a new way, many have proclaimed. Christianity is about to be accepted throughout the world, and a great revival establishing the kingdom of God will happen: then, and only then, can Jesus return, they say.

Obviously there are several ways to interpret the destiny of the church in the last days. My

---

11 . 2 Thessalonians 2:3-4.

12 . 2 Thessalonians 2:9–10.

view, based on the Scriptures, is that the last days
will be a time when Satan's agenda to deceive the
world will intensify. According to this
perspective, people who claim they are Christians
will actually be part of a scenario which promotes
a counterfeit gospel for a counterfeit Christ. It is
also my view that this grand delusion is already
underway.

NEW WINE OR OLD DECEPTION?

Over the past several years the New Wine
renewal/revival movement has been sweeping the
world. An experience-based Christianity
promoting a faith built on feelings and a desire to
seek after signs, wonders, and miracles continues
to spread like wildfire on a global basis. In spite of
the numerous scriptural warnings which indicate
that a time of great deception will come before
Jesus returns, a major sector of Christianity remains
committed to pursuing the idea that it is more
important to experience God than it is to know
His Word.

ANOTHER GOSPEL?

The issue we intend to examine in this book is
whether or not we could be living in a period of
history when the world is being prepared to
accept a man proclaiming that he is God. Is it
possible that even well-meaning Christians could
actually get caught up in the deception which

helps prepare the way for the Antichrist, as described by Paul in 2 Thessalonians?

Are we seriously paying attention to the warnings of Scripture which indicate that the last days will be characterized by Satan's greatest efforts to deceive all of mankind? Is it possible for Christians to believe they are actually taking part in evangelizing the lost, when instead they are being used as a vehicle of deception to promote "another gospel"?

LET'S BE LIKE THE BEREANS

I am convinced there is only one way to know the truth. If the Word of God is the truth, as Jesus claimed,[13] then we must use the Word as our basis to discuss what is happening to the church today. The Word also gives us insight into where the church will be headed if church leaders do not heed God's warnings.

Luke commended the Bereans because they were diligent about searching the Scriptures daily, checking out all they were taught to see if it lined up with the Word of the God.[14] This is not a time to base our views on the future of the church on a dream, vision, or personal conversation someone claims they have had with God. This is not a time to be seeking after "every wind of doctrine" or desiring to have our "ears tickled" or our "flesh

---

13. John 17:17.
14. Acts 17:11.

refreshed." This is a time to be serious about a faith that is biblically based—a faith that is built upon the foundation of the Word of God.

3

New Wine

Some say that Christianity is experiencing a paradigm shift. Others say that God is pouring out "New Wine," and Christians are being empowered and enlightened as part of a great revival that is sweeping the world. Whatever the explanation, there are now over 400 million people worldwide who call themselves charismatic Christians.[15] Most of them believe God is doing a "new thing." What is this "new thing"? Is it really *New Wine* or is it old deception?

A NEW THING?

Over the past several years a very obvious trend has been taking place in Christianity. In what some call a "Christian awakening," millions of people are emphasizing that signs, wonders, and experiences are being manifested as part of a last-days revival that is occurring before Jesus

---

15. "The Charismatic Christian Renewal Worldwide," *The Jerusalem Post*, January 19, 1996, p. 19.

returns. Often, a Christian perspective which emphasizes testing all things according to the authority of the Word of God is downplayed or even ignored.

What actually is happening? How do we explain this phenomenon? Is God doing something new? Or is the world being set up to embrace a false form of Christianity which is based on extra-biblical, supernatural experiences? Is it possible that what is happening today could be part of the *apostasy* Paul warned would arise in the last days?

EXPERIENCE SEEKERS

One of the characteristics of the present trend is the belief that experience is the most important aspect of Christianity. For example, consider the words of C. Peter Wagner, a professor of church growth at the Fuller Theological Seminary. In an interview with *Time*, he gave his opinion why charismatic meetings are so popular today. He said: "People don't go to listen to the services, but rather to be a part of it."[16] He continued: "We live in an exceptional time. Certainly in the history of the United States we have never seen such a frequency of signs and wonders."

THE TORONTO BLESSING

The Toronto Airport Christian Fellowship (TACF), formerly called the Toronto Airport

---

16. Ibid.

Vineyard, has become known as a mecca for people to experience "signs and wonders." Meetings that began in January of 1994 still continue every night of the week but Monday.

In order to describe the kinds of human behavior associated with this "blessing," we can quote from the Toronto Airport Christian Fellowship's homepage on the Internet. It states:

> The Toronto blessing is a transferable anointing. In its most visible form it overcomes worshipers with outbreaks of laughter, weeping, groaning, shaking, falling, "drunkenness," and even behaviors that have been described as a "cross between a jungle and a farmyard." Since the beginning of the outpouring on January 20, 1994, many people from our meetings have been affected in a number of ways: falling down under the power of God, becoming drunk in the Spirit, laughing uncontrollably or in some cases even roaring like lions.[17]

This strange behavior is interpreted by the promoters of the "Toronto Blessing" as a "divine visitation."[18] Thousands of pastors and leaders from around the world have traveled to Toronto and had the "blessing" imparted to them. They have then taken this "anointing" back to their own

---

17. Homepage for TACF on Internet.
18. Ibid.

churches, where the same kinds of behavior have broken out.

There are now literally thousands of "New Wine drinking holes" all over the world where hundreds of thousands of people are being "touched" every day. Catholics and Protestants from various denominations are claiming they are receiving the "gift of drunkenness" and being overcome by the "Spirit" as the "New Wine" empowers them to become part of the greatest revival ever known in the history of the world.

HOW DO WE KNOW THIS IS GOD?

Not everyone who has observed the "Toronto Blessing" believes it is from God. Some suggest the people who embrace it risk self-delusion or, worse yet, deception which is satanically inspired. Critics of the movement suggest that teachings that are not biblically based have the potential to open the door for satanic deception in the name of Christianity.

However, John Arnott, the senior pastor of the Toronto Airport Christian Fellowship and author of *The Father's Blessing,* is not the least bit concerned. He is convinced that the "Toronto experience" is part of a "heaven-sent renewal meant for the local church, in order to build up the body of Christ." Arnott also believes that "eventually it will overflow into the community and usher in revival."[19] He further stated in an interview that "God has told us to give the anointing away to whoever would like it, especially to pastors and elders who can bring it back to their churches."[20]

According to Arnott, an intellectual understanding of the Scriptures is secondary to having a loving emotional relationship with God. For example, in his book *The Father's Blessing* he states:

> It came as a tremendous revelation to me several years ago that the Christian faith is all about love and "romance" or intimacy. I used to think it was all about understanding the truth and getting our doctrine straight.[21]

As one reads through *The Father's Blessing*, it becomes apparent that Arnott is somewhat divided about the importance of doctrine as the basis for determining our Christian beliefs. On another page of his book he states:

> New doctrines need to be weighed very carefully. One thing that thrills me so much about this new outpouring of the Holy Spirit is that no new doctrines are being taught. There is nothing new here.[22]

---

19. Gail Reid, "After the Laughter," *Faith Today*, March-April 1995, p. 19.
20. Ibid.
21. John Arnott, *The Father's Blessing* (Orlando, FL: Creation House, 1995), p. 16.
22. Ibid., p. 37.

However, in the same book, Arnott completely contradicts himself by writing:

> Yet as we see the Spirit of God doing more and more, we may see some things that no chapter and verse in the Bible specifically describes. Why? God did not intend to describe every act He would ever do in the Bible.[23]

So what is Arnott actually saying? First, he states the so-called "Toronto Blessing" is scriptural and that it is not new. Then he turns around and attempts to justify his view that experiences cannot be restricted by biblical parameters.

BEING AN ANIMAL FOR JESUS

People who promote the New Wine movement say that you can't put God into a box. They believe that strange human behavior might be caused by God and we should be careful not to judge or criticize this behavior too quickly.

But what if someone makes sounds or behaves like an animal during a church service? Is this weird enough to say, "This couldn't be God"? What basis do we have to judge experiences? If there is no basis, does that mean that anything and everything that happens in a church is from God?

One of the ways that people are responding to this so-called "new blessing" is by manifesting strange animal behavior in the church. According to Arnott and others, this behavior is interpreted as

---

23. Ibid., p. 61.

having "prophetic significance." For example on page 178 of Arnott's book, *The Father's Blessing* we read:

> It is no coincidence that we have seen people prophetically acting like lions, oxen, eagles and warriors. In Steve Witt's church in St. John's New Brunswick, I saw all four of those manifestations happening all at the same time. The people who were doing this were mostly credible pastors and leaders. I was astonished but sensed the awesome presence of God. [24]

Arnott then goes on to describe what happened at the same church when a woman was overcome by the "presence of God" and began to prophesy. He writes:

> One lady who played keyboard and weighed about 115 pounds was on all fours, snorting and pawing the ground like an angry ox or bull. It was obvious that she was surprised and a bit frightened by what was happening, but at the same time she seemed determined to follow the Spirit's leading. For about an hour and a half this lady gave the most incredible prophetic word. She expressed the anger of the Lord against what Satan has done to God's church, His people, His cities, and communities. She said the powers of darkness were being pushed back and new boundaries were being set. [25]

---

24. Ibid., p. 178.
25. Ibid., p. 178.

Or consider the first-hand account of a man who observed the "ministry time" at John Arnott's own church in Toronto in the summer of 1995. He stated: "Two men were both on all fours, roaring at each other and gnashing at the crowd. Several in the crowd were cheerfully waving their hands in a scooping gesture as though they were flipping something through the air as they kept saying, "Give them more Jesus, give them more."[26]

Several minutes later the scene changed. The testimony continues: "Now the big lion had the little lion by the ankle and was roaring and grinding his teeth. Several enthusiasts were still saying, 'Give them more, Lord, give them more.'"[27]

GIVE THEM MORE OF WHAT?

John Arnott is not alone in his wholehearted endorsement of what he calls the "presence of God" in his church services. Many prominent leaders are equally enthusiastic about what they believe God is doing in Toronto. For example, Jack Hayford, senior pastor of the Church on the Way, endorsed Arnott's book by saying:

> John Arnott is seeking to provide a biblical soundness and a shepherdly care amid the mix of both the familiar and unfamiliar evidences of God's working at Toronto Airport Vineyard

---

26. Len Lindstrom, *News Report*, July 1995, p. 4.
27. Ibid.

[now the Toronto Airport Christian Fellowship]. [28]

Melody Green Sievright, president of Last Days Ministries, added her endorsement to John Arnott's book by saying:

John Arnott, with great humility, discernment and balance, brings understanding to the wonderful way the Father is refreshing His people today. [29]

Would John Arnott, Jack Hayford, Melody Green Sievright, or any other New Wine enthusiast please give the church a *biblical* explanation for what is going on? Where in the Bible can we find a basis for the kind of behavior now being claimed as a blessing from God? Since when can the Holy Spirit be "scooped," "flipped," "focused," or manipulated by human hands? Where in the Bible does it say that in the last days believers will act like animals in the church and that this should be interpreted to mean they are being used by God to speak prophetically?

If we are willing to base our theology and doctrines upon feelings, emotions, and unscriptural practices, then we have opened the door to a great delusion. The time to test all things scripturally is now. If we are not willing to do

---

28. John Arnott, *The Father's Blessing*, back cover.
29. Ibid.

that, then we are willfully choosing to be deceived.

A BLESSING OR A CURSE?

In 1 Corinthians Paul discusses the gifts of the Holy Spirit. These gifts are compared to the various parts of the body, which are all necessary as each part works together for the benefit of the whole. Although the gifts of the Holy Spirit are clearly described, some today insist that "new gifts" need to be added to the list. According to this view not all of the gifts that God has for us are in the Bible.

One of the ways that people can "receive" one of these new gifts is to go to a place where the "Spirit" is moving. Although John Arnott's Toronto Airport Christian Fellowship has been the main center of attraction, there are many other places where the Spirit has allegedly followed those who have been blessed at Toronto. Today there are many New Wine drinking holes.

Although the "Spirit" can be transferred in a variety of ways, John Arnott recommends a method known as "soaking." In his own words:

> We call this whole process of continuing prayer "soaking" someone. The person is getting soaked in prayer and in the Holy Spirit. This may go on for ten minutes or two hours. Soaking prayer seems to help people receive

more of God. We want to marinate them in the Holy Spirit.[30]

The "gift" of "being drunk in the Spirit" is another gift that New Winers promote. "Come and take a drink at Joel's bar and become drunk in the [S]pirit," enthusiasts say. "Don't try to figure out what God is doing! Just be open to whatever it is that God has for you. Don't try to figure out God— just let go."

"Letting go" is apparently one of the pre-requisites for the gift of "spiritual drunkenness" that so many Christians are boasting about these days. Interestingly enough, being "drunk in the Spirit" and being intoxicated by alcohol have similar characteristics. However, becoming drunk in the Spirit is supposed to mean that the person has received a blessing from God.

The justification that is used for the "gift of drunkenness" comes from Acts 2. Proponents of "spiritual drunkenness" say that on the day of Pentecost the disciples were accused of acting like drunkards, laughing, falling over, having slurred speech, and showing boldness with lack of restraint. However, the Scriptures state that it was the scoffers who suggested the people were drunk. The reason they said the disciples were drunk was because they were speaking in different languages—the gift of tongues. As any Bible

---

30. Ibid., p. 96.

student will tell you, the gift of tongues is in the Bible. However, the "gift of drunkenness" is not.

Nowhere in the Bible can we find that behavior resembling a drunken fool is something Christians should desire. In fact, drunkenness is associated with the judgment of God. For example, consider the words of the prophet Isaiah as he admonishes the people of his day who had rebelled against the Word of God. He stated:

> Stay yourselves, and wonder; cry ye out, and cry: they are drunken, but not with wine; they stagger, but not with strong drink. For the LORD hath poured out upon you the spirit of deep sleep, and hath closed your eyes: the prophets and your rulers, the seers hath he covered."[31]

Or listen to the words of condemnation by the prophet Jeremiah regarding what God would do to the rebellious people who refused to obey God's Word:

> And Babylon shall become heaps, a dwelling place for dragons, an astonishment, and a hissing, without an inhabitant. They shall roar together like lions: they shall yell as lions' whelps. In their heat I will make their feasts, and I will make them drunken that they may rejoice, and sleep a perpetual sleep, and not wake, saith the LORD.[32]

---

31. Isaiah 29:9–10.
32. Jeremiah 51:37–39.

It seems rather clear that behavior which can be compared to that of a drunkard is not a blessing—it's a curse. Is it possible that when Christians begin to seek after a power which is characterized by drunken behavior they are merely being deceived?

NEW WINE CONTINUES TO FLOW

On December 5, 1995, Vineyard movement leader John Wimber and several directors of the Association of Vineyard Churches traveled to Toronto, Canada to announce a decision they had made. For nearly two years, the Toronto Airport Vineyard had become known worldwide as the mecca for the experience called the "Toronto Blessing."

Supporters and even critics of the "Toronto Blessing" were shocked when news of the announcement came. The Toronto Airport Vineyard, which had become the focus of the New Wine movement, had been asked to leave the association of Vineyard churches. In other words, John Arnott and his church had been expelled.

When the news of the expulsion was released nearly everyone was confused. John Wimber had just endorsed John Arnott's newly published book *The Father's Blessing* by saying that he believed the senior pastor of the Airport Vineyard Church had been experiencing an authentic visitation from

God.[33] So what happened to cause John Wimber to change his mind?

As with every dispute and division that occurs in the church, there are always two sides. John Arnott, writing in the first edition of *Spread the Fire,* February 1996, explained his perspective of why the division occurred. He stated:

> The bottom line, we were told, is that the [Association of Vineyard Churches] Board felt the Toronto Airport Vineyard renewal services were not mirroring the Vineyard model. Rather than ask us to revamp the renewal meetings, they released us to continue as we believe God is leading us.[34]

Although this statement made it sound like the Toronto disassociation was congenial and without any major differences, a report sent out by regional director Happy Leman to Vineyard pastors to explain why the separation had occurred seemed to reflect another perspective. In a two-page statement, Leman wrote:

> The Association of Vineyard Churches and the Toronto Airport Vineyard seem to have fundamental differences in philosophy regarding the pastoral administration of this Renewal.[35]

---

33. John Arnott, *The Father's Blessing*, back cover.
34. John Arnott, "Here's Where We Stand," *Spread the Fire*, February 1996, p. 6.
35. Letter sent to Vineyard pastors in the Midwest Region by Happy Lehman, Regional Overseer,

Further, Leman pointed out other concerns that the Association of Vineyard Churches had with the so-called renewal that was being exported from Toronto. Some of these concerns included people being "hyped" or manipulated, an "emerging prophetic theology" that promoted an end-times "elitist mentality," abuses in behavior including "demonic activity," and the encouragement or spotlighting of "extra-biblical manifestations."[36]

Although many people thought that the expulsion of the Toronto Airport Vineyard by John Wimber would cause the "Toronto Blessing" to diffuse and finally go away, such has not been the case. People from all over the world are continuing to travel there seeking the same experiences that Wimber and his group were so concerned about. As well, the New Wine continues to flow within and without the Vineyard churches. In fact, Vineyard pastor Randy Clark from St. Louis, Missouri, has even exported the "Toronto Blessing" to places like Moscow.

THE MOSCOW BLESSING

In Russia it has been renamed the "Moscow Blessing." Although "the blessing" came via

Association of Vineyard Churches, December 8, 1995.

36. Ibid.

Toronto and is more commonly known as the "Toronto Blessing," now Russia has its very own version. Although the Moscow and the Toronto "Blessings" are different by name, there is a common denominator. Randy Clark is responsible for transporting the "anointing" not only to Toronto, but to Moscow as well.

The Izmylova Hotel in Moscow was the location where Randy Clark and his associates held their "Catch the Fire" conference. Over one thousand Russian pastors and church leaders were invited. Their expenses were paid by the promoters of the conference who had come from the United States. Before the conference, which occurred in the latter part of March 1996, there was some concern over whether the same manifestations associated with Toronto would happen in Russia. However, reports released on the Internet after the conference took place soon told the story.

From the very first night the Russians began to shake, shout, laugh, and roll on the floor. An Internet article reported that a typical scene was to see a husband and a wife "flopping on the floor like fish out of the water."[37] At the end of the meeting when the people were asked to leave, the report stated that "hotel officials directed those who were still able to walk to the conference exits.

---

37. http://www.grmi.org/missions/fsu/
russia.day1ii.html.

The remaining people were scooped up off the floor and escorted out. Most made their way back to their rooms, but several small groups of 'drunkards' made it no further than the main lobby where they staggered about and fell in heaps laughing."[38]

Another report issued after the three-day conference made it clear that the "Moscow Blessing" continued after Randy Clark and his "impartation" team left. Not only was the "blessing" taken back to various Russian churches, the "Moscow Blessing" took to the streets. An Internet report titled "Russian Fire Spreading" stated that people who attended the Randy Clark meetings "have remained drunk in the Spirit to the point of rolling around in the snow laughing. Pockets of people can be seen riding the Metro laughing and holding their stomachs from intense 'birthing cramps.'"[39]

BIRTHING CRAMPS?

He shouted "Fire" and hundreds of people fell to the floor. The scenario was not a firing squad— it was the Olympic Exhibition Center in London, England, where a large group of British pastors and church leaders had gathered to hear self-proclaimed Holy Spirit bartender Rodney

38. Ibid.
39. http://www.grmi.org/missions/fsu/
    russia.fire1.html.

Howard-Browne. Some have claimed God is using Howard-Browne to prepare the church for a great work that is still to come. A "new child" is being born, they say; just stand in line, "catch the fire" and be empowered.

Charisma, March 1996, reported this occasion as a landmark event in Great Britain. Hundreds of pastors and church leaders gathered in London to see and hear Howard-Browne. Although the "Toronto Blessing" had already been embraced in thousands of churches throughout Britain since May of 1994, now the man who had been credited with having lit the original fire was in town.

Certainly those who came to the meetings to "experience the experience" were not disappointed. Hundreds of pastors went forward and were organized into lines to receive prayer. Howard-Browne swept along the lines, shouting, "Fire." *Charisma* reported that it required an army of associates to run and keep up to him, trying to catch people who were falling over on the floor.[40]

Westminster Chapel minister R.T. Kendall was interviewed by *Charisma* magazine and gave Howard-Browne a rave review. "He's fearless," Kendall said of Howard-Browne. "When I met Rodney a year ago, I was touched by being in his

---

40. Clive Price, "Rodney Howard-Browne Wins Support from Church Leaders in England," *Charisma*, March 1996, p. 18.

presence." Then he continued, "The phrase 'baby-Isaac' just kept coming to me."[41]

So what is this idea, that a very large, full-grown man like Howard-Browne could be compared to "baby-Isaac"? What are the "birthing pains" that Christians are supposed to be experiencing?

The *Charisma* article answers that question. It states: "Kendall believes the church is in the embryonic phase of what could prove to be the greatest work of the Spirit since the days of the early church. [Kendall] believes that God has called Howard-Browne to initiate something big that is just beginning."[42]

A review of the charismatic literature reveals that Kendall's idea about the birthing of a new man-child or a "baby-Isaac" is not original. The idea has been around for a number of decades.

It's this theology of an "army of overcomers" and "baby-Isaacs" like Howard-Browne that many find deeply troubling. Some call this army of empowered Christians "Joel's Army." They believe that in the last days, a mighty army of Christians will be raised up and the world will be won for Jesus. As those who lived through the Latter Rain movement over forty years ago will remember, the "overcomers" doctrine did not

---

41 . Ibid.
42 . Ibid.

build up the church—it devastated it. Could history be repeating itself?

4
Winds of Revival
or
Winds of Doctrine?

Proponents of the New Wine movement are saying that tremendous signs of revival are in the air. All over the world an interest is being expressed in Christianity as never before. Certainly the gospel of Jesus Christ is being proclaimed as Jesus said it would before His return, and many people are genuinely becoming Christians.[43] But what about this idea that there will be a massive revival which sees the whole world accept Christ based upon signs, wonders, and miracles? Could seeking after experiences in the name of Jesus actually be part of a counterfeit gospel that could lead many people into deception?

---

43. Matthew 24:14.

THE MOVE IS ON

During the time of the prophet Joel, God brought judgment on the people of Judah by sending a terrible plague of invading locusts upon the land. The following words from Joel's prophecy describe the terror and destruction that occurred as a result of this invasion:

> A fire devoureth before them; and behind them a flame burneth: the land is as the garden of Eden before them, and behind them a desolate wilderness; yea, and nothing shall escape them. The appearance of them is as the appearance of horses; and as horsemen, so shall they run. Like the noise of chariots on the tops of mountains shall they leap, like the noise of a flame of fire that devoureth the stubble, as a strong people set in battle array. [44]

Although Joel clearly describes the horrible devastation that occurred as part of God's judgment during his lifetime, a growing number of Christians today believe this army of locusts is not an army of locusts at all. According to their interpretation of the Scriptures, the locusts described by Joel refer to Christians who are in the world today. These are the ones who are being empowered by New Wine to become part of a mighty army of God that will soon take over the world in preparation for Jesus' return.

---

44. Joel 2:3–5.

For example, consider the following interpretation of Joel chapter two by New Wine enthusiast Roberts Liardon. His book *The Invading Force* was published to exhort Christians to "take the strongholds of the enemy" as part of a mighty revival that he believes will take place before Jesus returns.[45] Liardon writes:

> In these verses of Joel, [Joel 2:7–11] we read of the great outpouring of the Holy Spirit in which we are now living. We are in the beginning of the greatest outpouring of the Holy Spirit the world has ever seen![46]

Then further expounding upon the aggressive nature of this so-called end-times army that he believes brings revival to the world, Liardon continues:

> This move of God is going to be very different from past moves, however, because it is going to "invade" people's homes and communities. The prophet Joel is talking about an army or a force, that cannot be stopped. He talks about an army that does not break rank. When the army—made up of you and me—invades, it wins. We are going to rule this earth for God![47]

---

45. Roberts Liardon, *The Invading Force* (Tulsa, OK: Albury Publishing, 1987), back cover.
46. Ibid., p. 7.
47. Ibid., p. 7.

REVIVAL DEFINED

Although to most Christians the word "revival" means a turning to God based on asking for forgiveness accompanied by a brokenness and a recognition of sin, the kind of revival talked about today by experience-based Christians is quite different. Certainly if it is possible to interpret the locusts from Joel 2 as empowered "born-again" believers, then it is possible to make the Bible say anything at all. And such seems to be the case.

Where in the Bible can we justify that in the last days a mighty army of God will take over the planet and rule this world for Jesus? In fact, where in the Bible does it even talk about a great revival of Bible-believing Christians who are fully committed to following Jesus Christ in the last days?

In order to better understand what is meant by the kind of revival that accompanies the Joel's army doctrine, it is important to quote Roberts Liardon once more. Answering the question, "What is revival?" he states:

> A revival is experiencing an intense presence of God on this earth. Revival is literally feeling the presence of God walking up and down the aisles of churches. A revival is when men come into contact with an invisible Being, and they cannot deny that there is a real, unseen Force called God in their midst.[48]

---

48. Ibid., p. 35.

EXPERIENCING GOD

The idea that revival is based on an intense presence of God "walking up and down the aisles of churches" is not unusual throughout Christian charismatic circles today. In fact, the New Wine theology promotes gatherings all over the world which are characterized by a vast variety of experiences which are interpreted as the "hand of God."

For example, a report by Rick Joyner discussing The Heart of David Worship and Warfare Conference held on April 18, 1996, on the east coast of the United States, reflects exactly what I mean. In this article Joyner described the atmosphere that was created the very first meeting. He writes:

> In the first meeting there was a holy electricity that charged the air. The worship immediately hit a level that was as strong as we have experienced, and immediately started pushing back the limits. There was no time left for a message or ministry, but it was right. We did not just want to talk about worship and warfare, we came to do it! Experience is a much better teacher than words. [49]

It is obvious that Joyner not only believes that experience is a better teacher than words, he also seems to believe that experience is a better teacher

---

49. pawn.spencer-davis.com [198.68.191.81] Friday, May 17, 18:23:19, 1996, p. 1.

than the Word of God. When one ignores the warnings of the Bible and desires to *feel* God based on experience alone, there is a great potential for deception. How do we know that a particular feeling was from God? How do we know it wasn't from Satan?

Joyner then goes on to give a detailed description of a sensual experience that occurred at The Heart of David Worship and Warfare Conference. He says:

> There was a presence of the Lord like I had never felt in a meeting before. I looked at Christine and Susy, who were dancing near the center of the stage, and I have never seen such a look of terror on the faces of anyone. An intense burning, like a nuclear fire that burns from the inside out, seemed to be on the stage. Christine started pulling at her clothes as if she was on fire, and Susy dove behind the drums. Then a cloud appeared in the center of the stage, visible to everyone, and a sweet smell like flowers filled the area.[50]

Certainly for Christine and Susy this experience was very real. But the question we should ask is, what was the source of this experience? Certainly Rick Joyner believed it was of God or he wouldn't have written about this encounter. However, as I have already stated, Joyner and other New Wine enthusiasts are not

---

50. Ibid., p. 2.

committed to evaluating experiences according to the Word of God. Their greatest desire is to *feel* God. As Joyner admitted in his own article: "I confess that I love the kind of supernatural manifestations that we have been having. I often pray that we will see His glory visibly manifested in our meetings."[51]

In this same article Joyner mentions that other supernatural manifestations besides "the burning" sensation are beginning to occur. He states:

> At all of our conferences now many are starting to see angels, and dreams and visions and prophecy are being released to people. This is all wonderful, and we are asking for more of it. We expect to see more and more miracles.[52]

However, it is apparent Joyner is still not satisfied with the intensity of the supernatural phenomena that have occurred so far. "We must go higher," he states. "Until we look like Jesus and do the work He did we still have not arrived. We must keep going for more. Much more."[53]

THIS IS GOD?

Reports and testimonies given by New Winers around the world demonstrate that more and more bizarre behavior is happening in the name of Christ. The phrase "being filled with the Holy

---

51. Ibid., p. 3.
52. Ibid., p. 4.
53. Ibid., p. 4.

Ghost" has taken on many new meanings. For example, consider the testimony of one lady who received the "blessing" after she was prayed for by a traveling evangelist from Argentina at a revival meeting at the Brownsville Assemblies of God Church in Pensacola, Florida. She states:

> He got me and all the prayer team members to line up against the walls of the back hallway. He went through praying, and in less than four minutes it was like the St. Valentine's Day massacre back there. Oh my goodness! I can not possibly explain, but it was like a bolt of lightening hit me and I hit the wall and slid down it and shook and jerked uncontrollably for I don't know how long. It took my breath away and I was taking deep gasps over and over. As each breath came in, my head would jerk to the back.[54]

The lady then went on to describe how the unusual jerking and breathing patterns continued uncontrollably as she drove home and then later on through the night. In her own words:

> This continued all the way home—I have no idea how I drove. I would start wailing out loud and then just grin a few minutes and then go back wailing. I feel like I was in intercession for loved ones about to attend the revival for the first time. When I walked in the door my husband thought I had been accosted in the

---

54. nw-news@grmi.org message ID 19960715021740733.AAA221@p. 5–133.

parking lot or something. I continued jerking and the extreme deep inhaling so much that I had to sleep on the couch. It was an awesome night. I would drift off and awaken with a big jerk! The breathing and the pushing back of my head have continued today, although not to the same degree. *Oh, I just love being filled with the Holy Ghost!* [emphasis mine][55]

BEYOND THE LIMITS

In spite of the warning issued by John Wimber and the Association of Vineyard Churches, New Wine experiences that go well beyond biblical parameters are still being promoted and show no signs of slowing down. Transferring the "gift of holy laughter" and the "spirit of drunkenness" still seem to be central to this "new move of God."

Although some New Wine supporters are concerned that these experiences are producing "spiritual addictions," there are few who are willing to correct the problem. British New Wine promoters Terry Virgo, David Holden, and John Hosier have written a book called *From Refreshing to Revival* in which they attempt to explain what the New Wine movement is all about and where they would like to see it go in the future. Commenting on the back cover of their book, they write: "It's amazing what people get up to in church these days—laughing, crying, leaping, falling, shouting and groaning. People are being

---

55. Ibid.

blessed. But what does it all mean? What happens when they get up off the floor?"[56]

According to Terry Virgo, people who are behaving strangely in churches are not acting abnormally, they are just "experiencing God's love."[57] Giving the usual argument to support the "gift of drunkenness" Virgo states:

> On the day of Pentecost the crowd thought that the disciples were drunk, and it's this sense of drunkenness that people are experiencing in this current move of the Spirit. They are no longer reasoning, "Yes, Jesus loves me, the Bible tells me so." They're saying, "I know that He loves me because I can hardly stand the intensity of it."[58]

Then Virgo continues his justification of the "gift of drunkenness" by describing what happened to a man who fell over and wept after he had been prayed for one night. He writes:

> Suddenly his weeping turned into laughter. He was rolling around completely drunk in the Spirit, overwhelmed by the love of God. That's so much more wonderful than telling someone, "Just read this verse and believe what it says."

---

56. Virgo, Holden, Hosier, *From Refreshing to Revival* (Eastbourne, England: Kingsway Publications, 1995), back cover.
57. Ibid., p. 68.
58. Ibid., p. 68.

There's nothing like the immediate activity of
God.[59]

BLASPHEMING GOD?

Seeking after an experience which requires no
biblical basis is well accepted these days in
Charismatic circles. People who limit God by
always checking out the Scriptures are told they're
"critical" and "putting God in a box." According
to this view, Christianity is undergoing a major
shift and God is "doing a new thing." Those who
do not open themselves up to the blessings are just
too analytical and unwilling to go along with the
"new move of God."

Since my previous book dealing with this
current wave of experience-based Christianity has
been published, *New Wine or Old Deception?* I
have been challenged by a number of people who
are upset because I have taken the position that the
"Toronto Blessing" is not a blessing. Some have
accused me of being too biblically based and that I
am "holding back revival." Others have said that
the rational position I advocate is dangerous and a
direct attack against the Holy Spirit. And even
others have said that I will be forever damned
because I have blasphemed the Holy Spirit.

Certainly being accused of "blaspheming the
Holy Spirit" is a charge which I have not taken
lightly. Of course, the assumption being made

---

59. Ibid., p. 68.

when people make these charges is that the strange behavior that has become known as a "blessing from God" is from the Holy Spirit.

Supporters argue they know this is a move of God because they have personally had the experience. Critics suggest that because there is no biblical basis for these "new gifts" we shouldn't assume that the behavior comes from God. In fact, they point out, the teachings that are being presented in the name of Christianity are the very things we should watch out for in the period of apostasy that the Bible states will happen before Jesus' return.[60]

CIVIL WAR IN THE CHURCH?

Some New Winers even go so far to say that the church is soon to be purged and that those who are not willing to go along with this new revival will eventually be eliminated.

Recently, Rick Joyner, who was quoted earlier in this chapter, published an article called "The Coming Civil War in the Church." In this publication Joyner points out that he believes a civil war is soon to break out within the church— a war which would be necessary to liberate a new breed of enlightened Christians who God was raising up. In his own words he states:

> There is a huge portion of the church which is being held bondage to the same religious spirit

---

60. 1 Timothy 4:1.

that manifested itself to the Pharisees, and it will attack any new movement that arises in the church. The more anointed the new movement is, the more these traditionalists will be threatened by it, and the more vehemently they will attack it. [61]

Joyner's solution to the problem of the people who are opposing this "anointed new move" sounds rather militant. He continues:

The longer we continue to compromise with such institutions, which use manipulation or control, for the sake of unity or for any reason, the more it will ultimately cost us to remove the cancer from our midst.[62]

Joyner then goes on to describe how he believes the conflict in the church will develop as two camps of Christians separate themselves into what he calls the "Blues" and the "Grays." He states:

The coming spiritual civil war will be between the Blues and the Grays. In dreams and visions blue often represents heavenly-mindedness, and gray speaks of those who live by the power of their own minds—which is equivalent to the brain's gray matter. This will be a conflict between those who may be genuine Christians, but who live mostly according to their natural

---

61 . From owner-awakening@pawn.spencer-davis.com, May 17, 18:51:21, 1996. Taken from Morning Star Prophetic Bulletin, May 1996.

62. Ibid.

minds and human wisdom, and those who follow the Holy Spirit.[63]

This spiritual elitism that New Winers are talking about is spreading worldwide. Although not everyone is familiar with Joyner's concept of the two camps—the Blues and the Grays— churches all over the world are now experiencing the fallout from this kind of divisive theology.

I am concerned where this idea of labeling Christians as Blues and Grays will end. During the Latter Rain movement of the 1940's, groups of people throughout North America were saying something very similar. This new breed of "spiritually enlightened believers" were the "Overcomers" or "Manifested Sons of God." Eventually these spiritually enlightened ones separated themselves from other Christians. Some even stopped praying to Jesus. They themselves had become so spiritual they considered themselves to be God! Is this happening again? Could this be a part of the apostasy that prepares the way for the man who says that he is God?

---

63. Ibid.

PART II

THE MAN
WHO BECOMES DIVINE

5

Could a Man Be God?

Apostasy is defined as "a falling away from the faith." Biblical faith is based upon hearing and believing the Word of God. Based on this definition, and the present trend that is happening in Christianity, apostasy is well underway.

However, a question remains to be answered: are we living in the period of time that Paul said would precede the man who would proclaim that he is God? Is this just some warped theological view that a few Bible-believing Christians teach in order to promote their own eschatological bias? How could anyone ever suggest that Christians who follow the name of Jesus could actually be a part of the delusion which would prepare for another Jesus—the Antichrist?

IT'S HAPPENING NOW

Throughout history many people have claimed to be God. Although we recognize that most of them were mere lunatics who had delusions of grandeur, many people walking around the earth today claim they have become God and are taken seriously.

The pathway to godhood is within the grasp of everyone, some are saying. For example, when Shirley MacLaine proclaimed her divinity over prime-time television by repeating over and over again—"I am God, I am God"—millions took her seriously. Or when the Dalai Lama of Tibet, the recipient of the 1989 Nobel Peace Prize, proclaims to the world that he is God, people of various faiths agree with reverence and enthusiasm.

What in the world is happening? How can these famous people get away with not being locked up in an institution for their outlandish statements? Do Shirley MacLaine and the Dalai Lama actually believe they are the equivalent to the God of the Bible? Or can the kind of godhood they are talking about be understood in light of the Bible?

THE ORIGINAL LIE

According to the Bible, the idea that a created being can become God originated in the heavenly realm before it was propagated here on Earth. In Isaiah 14 we read about the fall of Lucifer:

> How art thou fallen from heaven, O Lucifer, son of the morning! How art thou cut down to the ground, which didst weaken the nations! For thou hast said in thine heart, I will ascend into heaven, I will exalt my throne above the stars of God: I will sit also upon the mount of

the congregation, in the sides of the north: I will ascend above the heights of the clouds; I will be like the most High. Yet thou shalt be brought down to hell, to the sides of the pit.[64]

Most Bible scholars equate the fall of Lucifer with the fall of Satan. At this time one of God's created angels decided he would rebel against God and instead declare himself to be as God. When God created the earthly realm and Adam and Eve, the first humans, Satan appeared to Eve as a serpent and enticed her with much the same lie as had caused his own fall. Satan said:

Yea, hath God said, Ye shall not eat of every tree of the garden? And the woman said unto the serpent, We may eat of the fruit of the trees of the garden: But of the fruit of the tree which is in the midst of the garden, God hath said, Ye shall not eat of it, neither shall ye touch it, lest ye die. And the serpent said unto the woman, Ye shall not surely die: For God doth know that in the day ye eat thereof, then your eyes shall be opened, and ye shall be as gods, knowing good and evil.[65]

So the source of the idea that man can become as God is very clear. Satan, who the Bible calls the great deceiver, has a plan. If he is destined to the pit of hell for eternity, then he will attempt to do

---

64. Isaiah 14:12–15.
65. Genesis 3:1–5.

all he can to change God's mind by taking as many humans hostage with him as possible.

Certainly the last-days scenario will be no different. In fact, as we look through the Scriptures, it is apparent that the Bible does not teach that there will be a tremendous revival and a turning to Jesus Christ in the last days. In fact, the exact opposite is true. The two roads Jesus talked about in Matthew 7 still have not changed. The wide way leads to hell, and many are still traveling on it; the narrow way, which can only be accessed through a personal relationship with Jesus, is still the narrow way. Must we be reminded that there is only one gospel—the gospel of grace?

6

Who Is This Man?

In 2 Thessalonians, the apostle Paul prophetically describes the man who will claim to be God as a "man of lawlessness" and the "son of destruction."[66] Who is this man that Bible-believing Christians have always called the Antichrist? Is he a mere human being who is empowered by Satan? Will he appear at a time when the world is looking for a leader and world peace? Does the Bible give us any insight into who this man actually is and what he represents?

A MORE SURE WORD

The Bible is an amazing book. One of the things that proves the Bible is different from any other book is the fact that when it makes statements about the future, we can guarantee it will be one hundred percent accurate. And even more incredible is the fact that the writers of both the Old and New Testaments were inspired to

---

66. 2 Thessalonians 2:3.

write prophecies about similar events as they were moved by the Spirit of God. When it comes to investigating biblical revelation regarding the man who claims to be God, we see this is also the case.

DANIEL MENTIONED HIM

The Book of Daniel is one of the most studied Books of the Bible when it comes to understanding prophecy and end-time events. The visions that God gave to Daniel are accepted by most Bible scholars as a preview of many of the events that would take place after Daniel lived. These events would continue on until the last days including the days until the Lord returns.

No person who reads this part of the Bible can seriously cast it off as just a piece of literature that has no significant meaning. The Book of Daniel is clearly inspired. Much of what it predicts has already happened or is presently underway. What is yet to take place is just around the corner.

The prophet Daniel had something to say about the coming world leader that has not yet been revealed. Further clarifying Paul's warning to us in the Thessalonian account that the Antichrist will be an evil impostor whose objective is to deceive the whole world, Daniel declares:

> And he shall speak great words against the most High, and shall wear out the saints of the most High, and think to change times and laws:

and they shall be given into his hand until a time and times and the dividing of time.[67]

JOHN FORETOLD HIS COMING

For clarification of Daniel's statement regarding the Antichrist, we can turn to John's vision as recorded in the Book of Revelation. John writes:

> And they worshipped the dragon which gave power unto the beast: and they worshipped the beast, saying, Who is like unto the beast? Who is able to make war with him? And there was given unto him a mouth speaking great things and blasphemies; and power was given unto him to continue forty and two months. And he opened his mouth in blasphemy against God, to blaspheme his name, and his tabernacle, and them that dwell in heaven.[68]

Who can deny the inspiration of the Scriptures? What Daniel, Paul, and John foretold about the coming world leader who will claim that he is the Messiah, all coincide and agree. How soon will he be revealed? And how will the world know when he has appeared?

---

67. Daniel 7:25.
68. Revelation 13:4–6.

7
Signs of His Appearing

How and when will the Antichrist be revealed? These are the two most common questions asked by those who are avid students of Bible prophecy. Many candidates who have supposedly had the credentials to be the Antichrist have come and gone. Later these men turned out to be nothing more than mere humans who were endowed with or inspired by demonic power. What signs will prove for certain that the man Paul said would claim to be God has appeared? Will Christians be around to see this event?

THEY HAVE COME AND GONE

Hitler—Mussolini—Stalin—Gorbachev: the list goes on and on. "Pin the tail on the Antichrist" has long been played by those who believe the Bible teaches that a coming world leader will eventually claim to be God. History has revealed that when it comes to picking the Antichrist, until now all who have speculated have been totally wrong.

So what sign must be fulfilled to prove conclusively that the false Messiah has appeared? The Bible teaches that one of the feats that the Antichrist will have to perform is to rise from the dead in order to be an actual counterfeit of Jesus Christ. All genuine believers know beyond the shadow of a doubt that Jesus Christ died and rose again. However, many today, including the Jews, reject the resurrection of Jesus and are looking for their own Messiah.

In Revelation 13, John describes this man, who he calls the beast, by saying:

> And I saw one of his heads as it were wounded to death; and his deadly wound was healed: and all the world wondered after the beast. And they worshipped the dragon which gave power unto the beast: and they worshipped the beast, saying, Who is like unto the beast? Who is able to make war with him?[69]

So, according to the Bible, those who have rejected Jesus of Nazareth as their Messiah will accept this counterfeit Christ and worship him. One thing that many Christians are concerned about is whether they will be here to see the Antichrist in action. Is there any way of knowing?

This very question was clearly answered by the apostle Paul in 2 Thessalonians. Speaking of

---

69. Revelation 13:3–4.

the time when the Antichrist will be revealed, he states:

> Remember ye not, that, when I was yet with you, I told you these things? And now ye know what withholdeth that he might be revealed in his time. For the mystery of iniquity doth already work: only he who now letteth will let, until he be taken out of the way.[70]

Paul, writing to the Thessalonians under the inspiration of the Holy Spirit, made it clear that the Antichrist cannot be revealed until the Holy Spirit is removed from the world.[71] If the Holy Spirit is removed, this will mean that those who have been redeemed by the blood of Jesus Christ will be gone. Are you expecting to see the Antichrist appear? If you are a Christian and have the Holy Spirit living in you, it is plain and simple. You won't be here.

IN THE TWINKLING OF AN EYE

Today, the teaching of the rapture, or supernatural removal of the church from the world, is becoming less and less popular among Christians who profess to believe the Bible. Many New Winers who consider themselves part of the "Joel's Army" which is establishing the Kingdom of God are saying the rapture is an "escapist" doctrine accepted by those who have not been enlightened

---

70. 2 Thessalonians 2:5–7.

71. 2 Thessalonians 2:6–7.

to realize that man must prepare the way of the Lord by establishing the Kingdom of God here on earth. This view, known as amillennialism, reinterprets the Scriptures relating to the restoration of Israel and substitutes the church in Israel's place. Therefore, there are two definite camps of believers who are part of the church today—those who believe in the rapture and those who do not.

Paul clearly taught about this removal of believers in an event which he called a mystery. Writing to the Corinthians he stated:

> Now this I say, brethren, that flesh and blood cannot inherit the kingdom of God; neither doth corruption inherit incorruption. Behold, I show you a mystery; We shall not all sleep, but we shall all be changed, In a moment, in the twinkling of an eye, at the last trump: for the trumpet shall sound, and the dead shall be raised incorruptible, and we shall be changed. For this corruptible must put on incorruption, and this mortal must put on immortality.[72]

It is obvious from other Scriptures that this supernatural event, which transforms bodies in the twinkling of an eye, is not just for the dead, but also for those who are living when Jesus comes to receive His bride—the church. Paul further clarified what he was talking about when he wrote to the Thessalonians by saying:

---

72. 1 Corinthians 15:50–53.

For this we say unto you by the word of the Lord, that we which are alive and remain unto the coming of the Lord shall not prevent [precede] them which are asleep. For the Lord himself shall descend from heaven with a shout, with the voice of the archangel, and with the trump of God: and the dead in Christ shall rise first: Then we which are alive and remain shall be caught up together with them in the clouds, to meet the Lord in the air: and so shall we ever be with the Lord. Wherefore comfort one another with these words.[73]

SIGNS OF HIS APPEARING

If to be the Antichrist one must rise from the dead, are there other feats or accomplishments to be fulfilled to confirm his identity? Does the Bible give us any more clues about what this counterfeit Christ will actually say and do? Might we be living in the very era when he will appear and set up his reign?

According to John's vision, after three and one half years, the Antichrist will make the claim that he is God and blaspheme God and those who are God's children.[74] The prophet Daniel also stated that this man of iniquity will blaspheme God by setting himself up in the holy temple in Jerusalem, and from there claim that he is God.[75]

---

73. 1 Thessalonians 4:15–18.
74. Revelation 13:5–6.
75. Daniel 12:11.

UNDERSTAND THE TIMES

How far away are we from these events? Could they be in the foreseeable future? Is the world ready for a Messiah who has an answer to the world's problems? Is it possible that a man will appear in our generation and be endowed with supernatural powers and abilities that will cause people to accept him as God?

Remember, Bible prophecy has never been proven wrong. If the Bible says that a given thing will happen, it will happen. The question of when this takes place may be conjecture, but the fact that it will happen is absolutely certain. Although we must be careful not to make wild speculations and come up with dogmatic conclusions on how we think Bible prophecy will be fulfilled, Christians should be informed of the Bible's warnings about the last days.

Although the Bible teaches that believers in Jesus Christ will not be here to see the reign of the Antichrist, if his unveiling is not far off, we should already be able to see a number of the circumstances that will prepare for his appearance. Are these things occurring? If you have not noticed, then your head has been in the sand. Now is the time to wake up, look around, and get prepared.

8

The Prerequisite for Power

Throughout history a number of men have been possessed by the obsession to control the whole world. Although greed, power, and jealousy have been the main factors behind their ambitions to rule the planet, the Bible foretells a time when a man will successfully become a world leader. This man will be empowered by the very Devil himself. Are we living at a time when such a man could be revealed? What do the current events tell us?

GLOBAL PROBLEMS

We live in a period of history when the world faces problems of global magnitude. Every day when we read the newspaper or hear the news on radio or television, the same headlines bombard us over and over again. How are we ever going to survive even to the end of the twentieth century? Scientists, economists, and sociologists are saying the same things: either the human race comes up with a solution to make our planet a better place to live, or we are not going to make it. The time has come to leave our old ideas behind and open ourselves to new, revolutionary thoughts that will bring peace, prosperity, health, and wealth to the human race.

The Bible talks about a time of false peace and prosperity that is coming. This period of false peace that Paul talked about, which is followed by a season of God's wrath and destruction, will take place right after Jesus Christ, the groom, snatches away His bride to be with Him.

As the apostle Paul stated to the church at Thessalonica:

> But of the times and seasons, brethren, ye have no need that I write unto you. For yourselves know perfectly that the day of the Lord so cometh as a thief in the night. For when they shall say, Peace and safety; then sudden destruction cometh upon them, as travail upon a woman with child; and they shall not escape.[76]

These verses provide tremendous insight into the events to occur before the revelation of the coming world leader who claims to be God. As previously discussed, after the rapture of the church occurs, the Antichrist will be revealed. Following a period of false peace, there will be a time of terrible destruction. The reason for this judgment, as we will later see, is that the whole

---

76. 1 Thessalonians 5:1–3.

world will have been deluded into worshipping the Antichrist as the true God. The religion professed by this man will embrace ancient Babylonianism masquerading in the name of Christianity.

How close are we to a world leader heading up a global political system? Could it be soon? If you are not aware of what is happening in world politics, then keep on reading as we document the signs of our times.

EARTH CONFERENCE ONE

They came from around the world. For the first time in history, politicians from many nations, spiritual leaders from the world's religions, scientists, and educators, gathered to discuss the problems facing the world. Since Earth Conference One was held in Oxford, England in April of 1988, similar conferences have attempted to come up with a common vision for our planet. However, not all of the citizens of the world believe that these conferences will succeed in bringing true peace and well-being to our planet. Some Bible-believing Christians see these discussions as events which are actually preparing the way for the Antichrist.

Earth Conference One was an historic event with paramount significance for understanding Bible prophecy. For example, consider the following description:

They gathered from parliaments, senates, and assemblies; temples, churches and mosques; from laboratories, universities, and boardrooms. It was the first time that spiritual and parliamentary leaders had come together with scientific experts to confront the threats of the environmental crisis, nuclear war, famine, and disease. After five days of dialogue and contemplation the participants pledged to join forces to care for and protect the Earth and all its interdependent forms of life.[77]

IT'S AN OLD IDEA

Although this conference was unique in announcing publicly that a global system of government is necessary for our planet to survive, this was not the first time that such a concept had been entertained. The idea of a new world order that will provide the keys to resolving our global problems has been suggested many times before.

For example, consider the following statement taken from the *Humanist Manifesto,* first formulated in 1933:

We deplore the division of humankind on nationalistic grounds. We have reached a turning point in human history where the best option is to transcend the limits of national sovereignty and to move toward the building of a world

---

77. Anuradha Vittachi, *Earth Conference One: Sharing a Vision for Our Planet* (Boston, MA: New Science Library, 1989), back cover.

community in which all sectors of the human family can participate. Thus, we look to the development of a system of world law and world order based upon transnational federal government.[78]

Or consider what Nobel prize-winning philosopher Bertrand Russell once said: "Science has made unrestricted national sovereignty incompatible with human survival. The only possibilities now are world government or death."[79] And in 1983, Lord Beveridge stated: "World peace requires world order. World order requires world law. World law requires world government."[80]

WORLD GOVERNMENT OR DEATH

World government is the order of the day. The global crises facing our planet are numerous. Ecological problems are not confined to national borders. With the advancement of nuclear technology that threatens to destroy the planet, peace is not an option; it is a necessity. While parts of the planet have an abundant food supply, other regions are starving to death. Certainly laying

---

78. Paul Kurtz, ed., *Humanist Manifesto* (Buffalo, NY: Prometheus Books, 1984), p. 21.
79. Quoted in official brochure of the World Federalists Association.
80. Phillip D. Butler, *Parliamentarians for World Order, The Canadian Intelligence Service*, Vol. 33, No. 5, May 1983.

down our national pride and joining forces to unite the world for peace and prosperity cannot be that bad of an idea.

Perhaps joining globally and politically would be a good solution if the God of the Bible were brought into the picture. However, as we will see, such is not the case. When we ignore God and trust in our own human understanding, there will always be a serious price to pay.

THE PLAN

The State of the World Forum was held from September 27 to October 1, 1995. Once more world leaders were invited to discuss the future survival of planet Earth. This time the event took place on American soil in San Francisco. However, the host of the conference, who has his base in California, is not an American; he is the former head of the former Soviet Union—Mikhail Gorbachev.

When I received a copy of a brochure called Toward a New Civilization promoting the State of the World Forum to be held in San Francisco in the fall of 1995, I could hardly believe my eyes. Although I have been a student of Bible prophecy for many years, the significance of this event was overwhelming.

The list of guests and participants for the conference reads like the "who's who" of world politics, world religion, and world economy. Consider the following invited participants: former

President George Bush, former British Prime Minister Margaret Thatcher, former Canadian Prime Minister Brian Mulroney, Ted Turner, George Schultz, William Gates, Ted Koppel, Jacques Delors, Javier Perez de Cuellar, Paul Volker, Colin Powell, Maurice Strong, Carl Sagan, Al Gore, Richard Leakey, and Michael Murphy— among others too numerous to mention.

Upon receipt of the initial brochure announcing this historic meeting I contacted the Gorbachev Foundation in San Francisco by phone to request further information. The following statement summarizes the organization's goals and purposes:

> The State of the World Forum is a project of the Gorbachev Foundation/USA, an international non-partisan educational foundation created in 1992 to address the immediate challenges of the post-Cold War world and assist the process of building a global consensus for our common future. As such, the Foundation convenes innovative thinkers from multiple disciplines to generate substantive and in-depth international dialogue on the fundamental issues we face in the coming century.[81]

But perhaps the real mission of the Toward a New Civilization conference was best summarized by Vaclav Havel, the president of the Republic of

---

81 . Brochure, The Gorbachev Foundation/USA, April 3, 1995.

Czechoslovakia, who adequately defined its theme by stating:

> There are good reasons for suggesting that the modern age has ended. Many things indicate we are going through a transitional period, when it seems that something is on the way out and something else is painfully being born. It is as if something were crumbling, decaying, and exhausting itself, while something else, still indistinct, were arising from the rubble.[82]

According to Mr. Gorbachev himself, mankind is "entering into a new phase of human development." It is apparent, he claims, "that at this momentous juncture in history we are giving birth to the first global civilization. We must appreciate more deeply human unity and embrace more fully human diversity."[83]

How exciting it is to be living at this time! Will these so-called promises by world leaders bring about the utopian dreams they claim, or is our planet headed down the dead-end road of a global catastrophe that is predicted by the Bible? If I were not a Bible-believer, I would want to give it some serious thought.

82. Ibid.
83. Ibid.

9

The Mark of the Beast

For years Bible prophecy scholars have foreseen the coming of a leader who will head a one-world government which will, in turn, be in control of a one-world economy. In order for there to be a global economy there would have to be a one-world currency. How could this take place? In order for this to occur there must be a network of communications that will be able to link everyone, everywhere. A system of buying and selling will have to be implemented throughout the whole world. Are we living at a time in history when this could actually happen?

ANOTHER SIGN

The Book of Revelation is too difficult to understand, many say. There are so many different interpretations! Which one can you believe? The words are written as symbolic language and don't actually mean what they seem. These and other ideas are often used by those who refuse to accept that the whole Bible, including the Book of Revelation, is the inspired Word of God.

The Book of Revelation has much to say about the coming Antichrist, the "man who says that he is God." And as with other prophecies that have not yet been fulfilled, it should be possible for us to look at events now happening in the world around us and observe signs which reveal the return of Jesus Christ is at hand. With this in mind, consider one of the commands of the Antichrist, as John stated in his vision:

> And he causeth all, both small and great, rich and poor, free and bond, to receive a mark in their right hand, or in their foreheads: And that no man might buy or sell, save he that had the mark, or the name of the beast, or the number of his name.[84]

These verses are without question among those most commonly discussed by Bible-believers and skeptics. As recently as two decades ago, these verses were difficult to comprehend in relationship to the technology that existed at that time. However, today, such is not the case.

According to these verses, the Antichrist will impose a system of buying and selling that will require all who worship him to be active participants. No one on the planet will be able to buy or sell, no matter who they are or where they live,

---

84. Revelation 13:16–17.

unless they have the "mark." This mark will be positioned either on the right hand or forehead.

What is this system all about? How could the whole world be tied into a massive data base that will prevent people from buying or selling unless they willingly participated in the plan?

A CASHLESS SOCIETY

We live in a virtually cashless society. By this we mean that no actual funds are required to make most financial transactions. Now an electronic impulse can take the place of your signature; no cash changes hands. All items must have a bar code that can be passed by an electronic scanner to identify them for sale. You must have your own Personal Identification Number (PIN) to withdraw cash from an automated bank teller. These are just some of the realities we have grown accustomed to accepting as part of the "electronic funds transfer age."

The changes in the way we buy and sell have crept up on many of us unexpectedly. How convenient not to have to carry cash, traveler's checks, or a checkbook as we travel around the world. The plastic credit cards so popular in the 60's, 70's, and the 80's are being replaced by the electronic debit cards of the 90's to make life so much easier. Now banks, businesses, and customers can be certain that funds can change hands as quickly as an electronic signal can travel from the earth to a satellite and back to the earth again. It's as fast as punching in your PIN and saying, "I will."

Certainly satellite technology has made the world a much smaller place in which to live. Electronic funds transfer exchanges have made financial transactions fast, simple, and convenient. But do any disadvantages come with all of these modern conveniences? What if someone learns your PIN; could your bank account be in jeopardy?

The answer may offer a solution to the immediate problem but may also set up the world for the Antichrist's agenda as outlined in the Bible. In order for personal identification numbers to be more personal, rather than having to type them manually, why not record the number in a silicon chip that can be implanted in the tissues of the flesh? If this were done, a simple electronic scanner could identify you and your bank account, and you would never have to carry a plastic card or a wallet again.

Such a system is already in place for identifying animals like cats, dogs, and cattle. And it works extremely well.[85] Certainly such a convenient system would be just as effective with humans. And as a bonus, it would even control

---

85. Avid Microchip brochure, "A Simple Injection Means a Lifetime of Protection," Pettrac, Norco, CA.

the sale of illegal drugs, as all cash transactions could be monitored by a world computer.

Does such a scenario resemble what George Orwell foretold in his book *Nineteen Eighty Four*? Of course that year has come and gone, but the "Big Brother" system of control he wrote about sounds strangely similar to the Bible's description of the monetary system that will be implemented by the Antichrist. Are people today in the world being conditioned to accept it?

10

Preparing the Way

According to John's vision in the Book of Revelation, the Antichrist will demand the worship of all those who follow him. And if he claims to be the Christ, does this mean that he will insist that everyone be a Christian? Or could the religion of the Antichrist be based on Christian terminology while embracing other religious views as being valid?

THE NARROW WAY

A foundational principle of Christianity is that Jesus Christ is the only way to eternal life. Although many people profess that there are many ways, this contradicts Jesus' own words. Christianity is based on accepting the fact that the shed blood of Jesus is the *only* way we can come into the Kingdom of God![86]

---

86. John 14:6.

THE WIDE WAY

Given that the Antichrist will boldly claim to be the Messiah, what kind of a belief system would he embrace in order to be true to his name? It seems logical to me that the Antichrist, who is empowered by Satan, would have the ability to deceive his followers into believing that he is the Messiah, even though he represents everything that opposes Jesus Christ.

Since Jesus said there is only one way to God and that He is the way, we can expect the Antichrist to claim that there are many ways to God and that everyone can be God. In fact, he himself will say that he has become God.[87] Although this idea may seem somewhat bizarre to the older generation of today, a survey of high school and university students will show that their view of God is sympathetic to this kind of thinking. The view that a man can become God, or indeed that everything is God, is no longer a foreign idea. It is the very foundation of what is called New Age thought, which is based on an Eastern metaphysical world view.

RELIGIOUS UNITY

The Bible teaches that Jesus Christ is the head of the Church established here on earth.[88] Therefore it would be natural to expect the

---

87. 2 Thessalonians 2:4.
88. Colossians 1:18.

counterfeit Christ, the Antichrist, to attempt to establish his own counterfeit belief system. For this to happen he will have to establish a global religious system to prepare the way.

In his book *Global Responsibility: In Search of a New World Ethic*, author Hans Küng presents his case for a world government and a global religious system. Regarding the necessity for world leaders to make changes if the planet is to survive, he states:

> In recent years I have been increasingly convinced that the world in which we live has a chance of survival only if spheres of differing, contradictory or even conflicting ethics cease to exist. This one world needs one ethic. Our society does not need a uniform religion or a uniform ideology, but it does need some binding norms, values, ideals and goals.[89]

So what is this "new world ethic" that Hans Küng says is so necessary if earth is to survive? Is this message part of an agenda that has been in the making for years? Are human political and religious leaders being tricked into implementing a program that is authored by Satan in order to prepare the way of the Antichrist?

A further examination of Hans Küng's objectives will give a clearer indication of what he

---

89. Hans Küng, *Global Responsibility: In Search of a New World Ethic* (New York, NY: Crossroad, 1991) front flap of the book cover.

believes is required to save the world. As Director of the Institute for Ecumenical Research at the University of Tübingen Germany, he is an expert on world religions and the impact they have on society. His best-selling books include *On Being a Christian, Does God Exist?, Eternal Life,* and most recently, *Reforming the Church Today.*[90] The objective of *Global Responsibility: In Search of a New World Ethic* is to show that there cannot be an ongoing human society without a world ethic for the nations; that there can be no peace among the nations without peace among the religions; and that there can be no peace among the religions without dialogue between the religions.[91]

THE GLOBAL SOLUTION

Isn't it good to try and resolve our global religious problems with global religious solutions? Shouldn't the world's religions be encouraged to lay aside their differences and join together in a worldwide religious system that will promise peace, prosperity, and brotherly love? Who would ever refuse to embrace such a wonderful idea?

Had God not warned us in advance of the dangerous deception of this counterfeit utopian idea, we would have an excuse. But He *has* warned us!

---

90. Ibid., back flap of book cover.
91. Ibid.

11
The New Spirituality

If the Bible foretells that humanity is destined to move towards a worldwide religion that comes under the canopy of Christianity, how will it possibly happen? What circumstances must occur for the religions of the world to come together and agree to disagree? Is there some way that all religions and belief systems could find Christianity "common ground"? Is the world ready to accept a new religious ethic that everyone could embrace?

THE PARADIGM SHIFT

Over the past several decades the world has undergone dramatic political, economical, and religious change. New Agers call it the paradigm shift; Bible-believers call it the last days. Without question, the greatest change has been in the area of spirituality. During the 1960's, the majority of the world's intellectuals proclaimed that God was dead. Science and technology had explained God away. By the 80's many of the same people were beginning to change their minds. The byproducts of technology have the potential of destroying us, they said. Now we need to find a new hope to bring about utopia. That new hope, many now claim, is to believe that everything is God.

How could such a materialistic worldview change to a spiritual worldview so quickly? Are humans destined to be attracted to spiritual things? Are there two sides to the spiritual dimension— good and evil? How can we know what is right or what is wrong? Are all things relative depending on what you want to believe? Isn't it a good thing to accept there are many ways to God and just believe that all is one?

LET'S JOIN TOGETHER

Such are the reasonings of those who are attempting to unite the religions of the world into one big, happy family. According to Matthew Fox in his book *A Manifesto for a Global Civilization:*

> The ecumenical movement holds out for the human race our last great hope for redemption. No religion is complete in itself. And no spiritual tradition can ignore the diverse and beautiful ways in which God has become incarnate in other cultures, other human periods and other spiritual traditions. [92]

---

92. Matthew Fox and Brian Swimme, *A Manifesto for a Global Civilization* (Santa Fe, NM: Bear & Company, Inc., 1982), p. 42.

Fox, a former Catholic priest and now a zealous promoter of the ecumenical movement, has a burning desire to see all religions become one. We are told that it is vitally important for believers of every religion and even unbelievers to agree to disagree and come together in a common world ethic that will save the world. In the words of Hans Küng:

> A common world ethic therefore needs not only the great coalition of believers and non-believers; also and in particular it needs the special commitment of different religions. What would it mean if all the representatives of the great religions ceased to stir up wars and began to encourage reconciliation and peace between the people?[93]

The time for believers and non-believers, Christians and non-Christians to join hands has come, we are being told. It is not important what you believe; what is important is that you believe in something, the message goes. From a biblical Christian perspective, if that "something" that you must believe is not based on Jesus Christ, it will be your ticket to a lost eternity.

CREATION SPIRITUALITY

According to the Scriptures the last days will be a time of great deception.[94] This deception will

---

93. Hans Küng, *Global Responsibility*, p. 60.
94. Matthew 24:4–5; 1 Timothy 4:1; 2 Timothy 3:6–10.

not only affect those outside of the Christian church. Paul stated that it will specifically have an impact on the church.[95] If true biblical faith is based upon hearing and believing in the Word of God, then the last days should be characterized by an attack on the authority of the Word. A dilution of the truth characterized by extrabiblical ideas masquerading as Christian in terminology and experience should be expected.

Perhaps the word "experience" best defines the Trojan Horse that is being used today to subvert the foundations of the Christian faith. Countless books written by authors claiming to be Christian present a position which is hostile to the basic message of Christianity. In general, there are many people today who are oblivious to the teachings of Jesus Christ. Although they often quote the Bible verse by verse, they mix the Scriptures with the teachings of witches, shamans, Hindu gurus, and Buddhist monks who claim there are many ways to God.

For example, consider once more the words of Matthew Fox. In his book *The Cosmic Christ* he describes a future renaissance taking place in the Christian church:

> I foresee a renaissance, a rebirth based on a spiritual initiative, as the result of the outpouring of the Spirit. This new birth will cut through all cultures and all religions and indeed

---

95. 2 Thessalonians 2:3.

will draw forth the wisdom common to all vital mystical traditions in a global religious awakening I call "deep ecumenism."[96]

The subtitle of Fox's book is *The Healing of Mother Earth and the Birth of a Global Renaissance.* His objective is to meld the mystical beliefs of all religions together into a new form of Christianity which he calls "Christian mysticism."

What is this "new renaissance" that Fox is talking about? How can you combine Christianity and paganism? Where in the Bible are we instructed to call the earth our "mother"? Where in the Bible do we find the justification to draw from the wisdom of all of the world's religions? This is not Christianity; this is apostasy in its most obvious form.

This Christian mysticism that Fox labels the "new birth" or "creation spirituality" is not new. It is the age-old consequence of rejecting the Creator and worshipping the creation. It is a revival of ancient Babylonianism. And for such a lie the wrath of God is reserved![97]

Bible-believing Christians should have no problem in recognizing the blatant deception that is being pawned off to the world in the name of Christ. However, as demonstrated earlier,

---

96. Matthew Fox, *The Cosmic Christ* (San Francisco, CA: Harper & Row, 1988), p. 5.
97. Romans 1:18–25.

Christians are not immune to deception. If apostasy in the church is one of the signs that the "man of perdition" is about to be revealed, should we not expect to see deception in the church interwoven with the deception in the world? Is it possible we are living in an era when a counterfeit form of Christianity is preparing the way for the counterfeit Christ?

PART III

NEW WINE
AND
THE MAN WHO
BECOMES DIVINE

12
The Third Wave

Many today believe that Christianity is entering a unique era characterized by the greatest revival the world has known. Commonly called the "Third Wave," the strange physical behavior now happening in many churches is supposed to indicate that a final great revival is here.

What about this Third Wave idea? Should we all jump on our spiritual surfboards and go for the ride? Is the Third Wave doctrine biblically based? Who are some of the promoters, and what is their agenda?

CATCH THE WAVE

Rodney Howard-Browne is known around the world as the man God has chosen to distribute the new "gift of holy laughter." According to Howard-Browne and his many supporters, holy laughter is a sign that the Third Wave is finally here.

The Coming Revival is a book written by Howard-Browne documenting his views on this

"revival" he claims has begun. Using surfing
terminology, the reader is encouraged to "ride the
wave." Howard-Browne also suggests that it is
important for participants to "read the wave" in
order to make sure that it is the "right wave." As
soon as this wave is over, Howard-Browne
advises people to look for successive waves that
will continue to come. According to this view,
one's ability to "catch the wave" is a reflection of
one's spiritual sensitivity. This "Third Wave," the
New Wine supporters claim, is producing a "new
breed" of Christian that is being prepared to take
over the planet and set up the Kingdom of God.

The Third Wave is not an original idea with
Howard-Browne. In fact, the concept has been
floating around the church for several decades.
According to this view, the "First Wave" occurred
in the early 1900's and was known as the
Pentecostal movement. It was limited to only a
small number of people in a few places. The
"Second Wave," described as the Charismatic
movement, affected more people in several
denominations, in a few countries. The Third
Wave, according to this scenario, is a final wave
that flows over the whole world before Jesus
returns. Powerful spiritual forces are supposed to
be unleashed, and signs and wonders will be
influential in converting the majority of the world
to Christianity.

Regarding this time when the Third Wave is
fully manifested, John Wimber is quoted as saying:

There will be a time where even as in Acts 2, suddenly, as they were gathered, in the midst of them, the Lord came and with an anointing beyond anything that has ever been given to man before. Something astounding, so marvelous that God has kept it a mystery as it were, behind His back, and He is about to reveal it. With the judgment of all mankind will come this incredible incarnational endowment of God's Spirit and we will see the Elijah's...this end-time army will be made of the Elijah's of the Lord God.[98]

THE LATTER RAIN

John Wimber's theology, which supports the idea that a mighty end-times army will be made up of empowered Christians, sounds very familiar. In fact, not only is it familiar, the very words that John Wimber has chosen to describe Third Wave empowered Christians are those that were used by the founding fathers of the Latter Rain movement some fifty years ago.

In *New Wine or Old Deception?* I documented this movement, which originated in North Battleford, Saskatchewan in the late 1940's. The connection between the "Toronto Blessing" and the Latter Rain movement was also documented. Although I do not intend to repeat what has already been written, it is important to understand

---

98. Bill Randles, *Weighed and Found Wanting: Putting the Toronto Blessing in Context*, p. 65.

that the "Third Wave outpouring" that is presently being promoted is clearly connected with the earlier "New Order of Latter Rain" beliefs and practices.

Although the "New Order of Latter Rain" seemed to dissipate after it was officially disapproved by the Assemblies of God General Council meeting in 1949,[99] the heretical teachings of this movement continue to influence many people to this very day. According to Richard Riss, a staunch Latter Rain enthusiast and author of a book called *The Latter Rain*, a "widespread underground movement developed within the Charismatic Renewal, composed of individuals committed to various 'end-time truths' that had arisen during the 'Latter Rain revival.'"[100]

To clarify, Riss quotes J. Preston Eby, a Latter Rain promoter, on page 143 of his book. Eby believed Latter Rainers who were empowered by the "Second Wave" would give rise to a "Third Wave." He stated:

> All of this [second wave] is being laid upon a people who have received the fruit of that great second visitation of God and thus they are being prepared for the coming third outpouring which shall bring fullness, a company of

99. Assemblies of God in the USA, 23 General Council Minutes (Seattle, WA: 1949), pp. 26–27.

100. Richard Riss, *The Latter Rain* (Mississauga, Ontario: Honeycomb Visual Productions, 1987), p. 143.

overcoming Sons of God who have come to measure the fullness of Christ to actually dethrone Satan, casting him out of the heavenlies, and finally binding him in the earthlies, bringing the hope of deliverance and life to all families of the earth. This third great work of the Spirit shall usher a people into full redemption—free from the curse, sin, sickness, death and carnality. [101]

BABEL AT A DISTANCE?

J. Preston Eby's statement was made as part of his Kingdom Bible Study in September of 1976, and clearly represented the Latter Rain eschatology which many still embrace. However, not everyone who supported the Latter Rain movement of the past remained as enthusiastic as Eby. For example, the following are the words of George Hawtin, one of the Latter Rain's founding fathers, as he looked back and commented on the things he had formerly embraced. He stated:

I shall never cease to thank God that I was vomited out of the belly of this whale also, for we never know the depths to which we have sunk until we are able to view Babel at a distance. Then and only then our heart gives

---

101. J. Preston Eby, *The Battle of Armageddon*, Part IV, Kingdom Bible Study, September 1976, p. 10.

thanks to God for deliverance from another of the harlot daughters of Babylon.[102]

George Hawtin's statement is particularly interesting in connection with the revival of the Latter Rain teachings today, which are part of "the new thing" that God is supposed to be doing. I am reminded of the words written by Solomon in the Book of Ecclesiastes thousands of years ago: "The thing that hath been, it is that which shall be; and that which is done is that which shall be done: and there is no new thing under the sun."[103]

The words Hawtin used to describe the belief he formerly held as the "harlot daughter of Babylon" are also very significant. In Revelation John wrote about a vision God had given him in which he used the words "Babylon" and "harlot"[104] to describe an end-times counterfeit church that would be the religious system endorsed by the Antichrist.

Could history be repeating once more? Could history be repeating for the last time? Could the Third Wave be a part of a religious movement that helps a man to declare that he is God?

---

102. George R. Hawtin, *Mystery Babylon* (Battleford, Saskatchewan), pp. 10–11.
103. Ecclesiastes 1:9.
104. Revelation 17:1–6.

13

Evangelicals and Catholics Together

As we approach the end of another millennium, a number of people are excited about the concept of global evangelization as Christians agree to unite based on common beliefs. Christians have been fighting among themselves for centuries. Now is the time for everyone who professes the name of Christ to join together and become one big happy family, they claim. Although the Bible does teach that love, brotherhood, and unity are the earmarks of those who follow Jesus Christ, is it possible that a quest for unity can go too far? What if the desire for ecumenical unity means turning our backs on the truth? Are we still willing to agree to disagree when the eternal destiny of mankind is on the line?

POWER EVANGELISM

The term "power evangelism" was coined by John Wimber. *Power Evangelism* is also the name of a book authored by John Wimber and Kevin

Springer, first published in Great Britain in 1985. This view of evangelism is predicated upon the supposition that the gospel message in itself, is largely ineffective unless accompanied by miraculous "signs and wonders."

In order to understand the concept of "power evangelism" Wimber and Springer claim it is important for Westerners to modify their world view. According to the authors, people who live in "third world countries" are more open to God's power because they have different beliefs and expectations. The Western, materialistic world, they believe, has held people back from experiencing the miraculous. For example the authors state:

> Most Western Christians must undergo a shift in perception to become involved in a signs and wonders ministry, a shift towards a world view that makes room for God's miraculous intervention. It is not that we allow God's intervention: he does not need our permission. The shift is that we begin to see his miraculous works and *allow* them to affect our lives.[105] [emphasis in the original]

Although Wimber and Springer say that God is sovereign in the previous statement, this view is not consistent with what is presented in other parts

---

105. John Wimber with Kevin Springer, *Power Evangelism*, Fully Revised With Study Guide (London: Hodder and Stoughton), p. 147.

of their book. The authors seem to suggest that "signs and wonders" can be induced in the West when a particular methodology is used. They state that Jesus actually taught His disciples how to perform signs and wonders:

> But Christ's method of training is difficult for Western Christians to understand. There are several reasons for this. Evangelicals emphasize accumulating knowledge about God through Bible study. Christ was more action oriented; His disciples learned by doing as He did. [106]

Wimber and Springer make another important statement explaining why Jesus' disciples were able to perform miracles. They write:

> He trained them to do signs and wonders. They were hitched together for three years, and when released, the disciples continued to walk in his way. They performed signs and wonders and trained the next generation to perform them also. [107]

Did Jesus really "train" His disciples to "perform" signs and wonders? Such a statement assumes that humans are able to bypass the sovereignty of God and can learn to initiate and imitate God's power by some method.

---

106. Ibid., p. 191.
107. Ibid., p. 195.

SIGNS AND UNITY

In 1992, *Power Evangelism* was reprinted in England, fully revised and complete with a study guide. According to the authors, this popular book, which had sold nearly 250,000 copies, needed to be rewritten "for clarity and easier reading."[108] As well, there were some entire sections that needed to be dropped from the revised edition. One of the sections that was eliminated was the area dealing with the Third Wave.

In the introduction to the revised edition, Wimber and Springer mentioned they dropped the Third Wave material because it is "now an historical fact for most Christians."[109] However, in the latter part of the book there is a brief discussion about the Third Wave, apparently written for readers who are still not familiar with the concept.

In "Appendix C," Wimber and Springer state that it was "C. Peter Wagner who coined the term 'Third Wave.'"[110] They also quoted what Wagner mentioned about the Third Wave in the January 1986 issue of *Christian Life* magazine:

---

108. John Wimber with Kevin Springer, *Power Evangelism*, Fully Revised With Study Guide (London: Hodder and Stoughton), p. 15.
109. Ibid., p. 16.
110. Ibid., p. 245.

> The term "Third Wave" has been with us about three years. It seems to have caught on to a considerable degree. People now know we are not referring to Alvin Toffler's new book of the same name, but to the Third Wave of the power of the Holy Spirit in the twentieth century.[111]

For those not familiar with Alvin Toffler, his views are typical of other New Age authors who take an evolutionary position that mankind is on the verge of entering a new era of enlightenment. New Age proponents believe that a higher level of consciousness is available to all those who are willing to open the door to this dimension through various Eastern metaphysical religious techniques.

Wagner is correct in suggesting that the term "Third Wave" did not originate with Alvin Toffler. However, he failed to mention that the Third Wave idea, as it relates to Christianity, actually originated in 1948 with the extrabiblical teachings propagated by the New Order of the Latter Rain. Such teachings as the Overcomers doctrine and the Manifest Sons of God doctrine, not only divided many churches, but left them in spiritual ruins.

However, the Third Wave which Wagner says originated in 1983, is not characterized by division. In fact, this Third Wave is based on

---

111. Ibid., p. 245.

unity. As he states: "One of the characteristics of the Third Wave is the lack of divisiveness."[112]

As well, Wimber and Springer also stress the importance of "unity" in regards to the effectiveness of "power evangelism." They state: "True unity among Christians will come only when issues that divide them are addressed."[113]

UNITY IN THE SPIRIT?

A casual reading of popular charismatic magazines today will reveal that the "Toronto Blessing" and other supernatural experiences are joining a variety of believers. For example, the October issue of *Charisma* magazine stated that a "refreshing from the Lord," at the Brownsville Assembly of God in Pensacola, Florida has become a gathering place for people of all denominations to receive "the gift of holy laughter" along with other physical blessings. According to John Kilpatrick, the church's senior pastor, these experiences (which he calls a "refreshing from God") have drawn people from various groups, including "Mormons, Catholics, Baptists, Jews, Methodists, Episcopalians, non-denominational and Greek Orthodox believers, as

---

112. Ibid., p. 246.
113. Ibid., p. 246.

well as Pentecostals from within and without the area."[114]

In another issue of *Charisma* we read that a revival is taking place in Britain which is also based on "laughing" and "spiritual drunkenness." Such experiences are uniting Anglicans, Methodists, Pentecostals, Baptists, and Catholics in Britain.[115] Without a doubt, an experience-based Christianity is being well received world-wide. Although there is no biblical basis for this kind of human behavior, advocates of an experience-based Christianity believe that it is "just people responding to God."[116]

ORLANDO 95

Certainly an ecumenical unity based on the common goal of pointing people to the finished work of the cross would be a noble effort! However, the present trend within Christianity indicates that this is not the case—common experiences seem to be the unifying factor. For example, consider what took place during the evening sessions at the Orlando 95 Conference, as Catholic and Protestant charismatics abandoned their differences and worshipped together:

---

114. Alice Crann, "Revival Stirs Florida Panhandle Church," *Charisma*, October 1995, p. 20.
115. *Charisma*, November 1995, p. 54.
116. *Charisma*, February 1995, p. 26.

Haitian Catholics danced conga-style in the aisles singing wildly in Creole. Robed monks and nuns skipped in the aisles along with Pentecostals, Methodists, Mennonites and Episcopalians. Others praised God by dancing around the convention center waving open umbrellas—perhaps to signify that the invisible rain of the Holy Spirit was falling.[117]

The Orlando 95 Conference was addressed by a number of key leaders who all were enthusiastic about this ecumenical gathering. These included Catholic Bishop Sam Jacobs, healing evangelist Benny Hinn, and Pentecostal Bishop Gilbert Patterson. Each speaker urged churches to work together. John Buckley, a Catholic priest from Tampa, Florida, said the conference had broken down walls of prejudice between believers. "This is the greatest ecumenical movement in the Christian church," he said.[118]

THE WALLS ARE DOWN

On March 29, 1994, a document was signed by forty religious leaders which, in effect, declared the Protestant Reformation of the 16th century a terrible mistake. This agreement has the potential of redefining the very essence of what it means to be a Christian. According to the agreement—called "Evangelicals and Catholics Together: The

---

117. J. Lee Grady, "Catholics and Protestants Join Forces," *Charisma*, October 1995, p. 26.
118. Ibid., p. 28.

Christian Mission in the 3rd Millennium"—
Catholics and Protestants should join hands, agree
to disagree on their differences.

Although in principle such an agreement
sounds good for the purpose of resolving our
social woes, what about the possibility that joining
hands socially and experientially may lead us to
compromise the true gospel of Jesus Christ? In
Paul's day, the Galatians were exhorted because of
their willingness to mix the finished work of the
cross with a system of works. When the Galatians
compromised the gospel Paul told them they had
been "bewitched."[119] So what about today? Has
the gospel changed, or are people still under the
same influence that deceived the Galatians some
two thousand years ago?

Protestants and Catholics standing together on
social issues may be a just cause. However, where
will this new brotherhood of believers end? We
have already seen how experiences like "laughing
in the Spirit" and "being drunk in the Spirit" can
join Catholics and Protestants and even Mormons
together, so where will this all lead?

MARY MAKES A COMEBACK

Ever since the *Evangelicals and Catholics
Together* document was signed by prominent
Christian leaders such as Chuck Colson, Pat
Robertson, and Bill Bright, advocating that

---

119. Galatians 3:1.

Catholics and Protestants should "agree to disagree," some interesting developments have occurred. It seems that some Protestants have not only relaxed their views on certain issues, but are willing to completely change their views and embrace Catholic doctrine.

One such person is Rev. Mark Pearson, president of the Institute for Christian Renewal and rector of Trinity Church, Plaistow, New Hampshire. He is a theologian affiliated with the Charismatic Episcopal Church. In an article called "Who Is the Virgin Mary" which appeared in *Charisma* he wrote:

> Though Roman Catholics often place too much importance on Mary, it's too bad that Protestants tend to ignore her. We have much to learn from the mother of the Christ child.[120]

Pearson further clarified his position by stating the following:

> Some doctrines about Mary held by the Roman Catholic Church may not necessarily be wrong. In many cases the biblical witness is not that clear or it's silent.[121]

Then justifying Catholic doctrine centered around Mary, Rev. Pearson stated:

---

120. Mark Pearson, "Who Is the Virgin Mary," *Charisma*, December 1996, p. 63.
121. Ibid., p. 66.

First, the assumption of Mary could have happened. It happened to Enoch and Elijah for sure and possibly to Moses. Second, Mary could have been a virgin perpetually. Reformers thought so. Biblical scholars are divided on whether the Greek word for Jesus' "brothers" (as in Matthew 12:48) means biological brothers or could mean close relatives. [122]

Then reconfirming that the goals of the *Evangelicals and Catholics Together* document are being established, Pearson stated:

There are signs that Christians across the Protestant-Roman Catholic divide are starting to listen to each other and jointly go back to the Scriptures. Who would have believed years ago that there ever would have been a Roman Catholic charismatic, much less millions of them? Who would have thought that in the "convergence movement" Pentecostal pastors would embrace liturgical worship and a higher view of the sacraments? Who would have imagined that David du Plessis not only would visit the Marian shrine in Medjugorje but also proclaim how much he liked it? [123]

Although Rev. Pearson says that ecumenical unity is happening because Catholics and Protestants are jointly going back to the Scriptures, is this really the case? Although Mary does

---

122. Ibid., p. 66.
123. Ibid., p. 66.

deserve special recognition because she is the mother of Jesus, when the Bible is silent on an issue, what gives anyone or any group the right to establish a doctrine based on what the Bible does not say? Catholics believe that Mary appears at Medjugorje as a messenger with new revelation from God to man. Where is that found in the Scriptures?

SPIRITUAL PILGRIMAGES?

A quarter-page advertisement in *Charisma* alongside an article called, "Catholics and Protestants Join Forces," seems to indicate where "Christian unity" is headed. A free 1996 Spiritual Pilgrimages brochure advertised by a Catholic organization called the Queen of Peace Ministry, offered tours to various places including Fatima, Guadalupe, and Medjugorje.[124] Although these places are claimed to have Christian significance by the Catholic Church, the occultic satanic practices that take place there are clearly anti-christ. Could agreeing to disagree with Catholics for the sake of becoming ecumenical partners be deceptive? Could people who sincerely believe in the gospel of grace be drawn into accepting a compromised gospel which emphasizes super-natural experiences in the name of Christ?

---

124. J. Lee Grady, "Catholics and Protestants Join Forces," *Charisma*, October 1995, p. 27.

14

"Christians" and Pagans Together

The "Evangelicals and Catholics Together" document may go down in history as the most significant ecumenical agreement of all time. Who would have thought this possible a few decades ago? Certainly Reformers like Martin Luther and John Knox, who dedicated their lives to advancing the gospel of grace, would not be able to comprehend what has happened if they were alive today. While it is important for Christians to forgive and forget about what has happened in the past, it is important to point out the gospel by grace alone has not changed.

A UNITED CHURCH

While Catholics and Evangelicals are signing documents and joining together for the sake of ecumenical unity, Catholics and other Protestants are joining with pagans and embracing their religious beliefs. "There is so much wisdom to be learned from these other religions," some Christian leaders say. It looks as though the trend to build a Kingdom of God in order to establish a new one-world church is here to stay.

For example, consider the following words of Pope John Paul II as he spoke to a large Hindu audience in India in 1986:

> India's mission is crucial, because of her intuition of the spiritual nature of man. Indeed India's greatest contribution to the world can be to offer it a spiritual vision of man. And the world does well to attend willingly to this ancient wisdom and to find enrichment of human living.[125]

This amazing endorsement of Hinduism by Pope John Paul II is only one of many statements he has made regarding the importance of becoming spiritual brothers and sisters with pagans. Speaking to Shintoists and Buddhists in Tokyo in 1981, John Paul II commended their spiritual traditions by saying, "I express my joy that God has distributed these gifts among you."[126]

THE NEW PROTESTANTS

In order to present a fuller picture of what is happening in this scramble for ecumenical unity, it

---

125. Pope John Paul II, "Spiritual Vision of Man," *L'Osservatore Romano*, February 10, 1986, p. 5.
126. Abbe Daniel Le Roux, *Peter, Lovest Thou Me?* (Instauratio Press, 1989), p. 45.

is important to point out that Protestants are just as enthusiastic to discover the "wisdom" found in pagan beliefs. For example, consider some of the classes being taught at the Naramata Center, a retreat facility operated by the United Church of Canada. The United Church is one of Canada's mainstream Protestant denominations formed by the unification of Methodists and Presbyterians several decades ago. According to a recent brochure outlining the Center's program:

> In faithfulness to the life and teachings of Jesus, guided by the voices of the Spirit and living in God's community, the Naramata Center is a place of learning, healing, and retreat for the empowerment of persons, for the renewal of relationships for the work of justice.[127]

Although the United Church leadership may claim to be true to the teachings of Jesus Christ (and that their denomination is therefore "Christian") a brief overview of some of the current teachings embraced by the United Church, cause one to wonder.

One of the courses taught at the Naramata Center is "Union and Communion with God." According to the course description in the Naramata brochure, the "experiential workshop will focus on grounding—being fully at home in one's body, the healing power of laughter and

---

127. Programs at the Naramata Center brochure, The United Church of Canada, January 1996, p. 2.

play, sacred earth walks, self-massage and spiritual sexuality."[128] The course instructor lives a "universal spirituality, which overlaps Eastern, Western and Native American traditions."[129]

Or consider another of the courses, called "Crisis in Ecumenism," which redefines Christianity altogether. The course outline states: "The United Church has attempted to set forth a new imperative: to work in partnership with people of other faiths and of no explicit affiliation, to heal the creation." It then asks, "Will 'whole-world ecumenism' rekindle the ecumenical fire and accomplish God's will?"[130]

CATCHING THE ECUMENICAL FIRE

In the July 1996 issue of *Charisma* an article called "Roman Catholics Embrace Renewal" claims that Monsignor Vincent Walsh of Philadelphia believed that evangelist Rodney Howard-Browne had revolutionized his parish ministry. The "revival fire" that he experienced after visiting one of Howard-Browne's meetings brought a deep change to his life and many of his parishioners. "We're in revival," Walsh said. "The Spirit's fire was growing all over the world and I

---

128. Ibid., p. 10.
129. Ibid.
130. Ibid.

wanted to catch some of this for the Catholic Church."[131]

The article also mentions Walsh's belief that his parish was one of the first Catholic groups to minister "revival fire"—the gift of holy laughter that he had received from Howard-Browne. "We hope what God does in our midst will touch the whole church," the priest said.[132]

DON'T WORRY—BE HAPPY

So what are we to make of these revolutionary ideas now being proclaimed in the name of Jesus? Will incorporating such daily sensual activities as laughing, self-massage, sacred earth walking, and becoming more sexually in tune, produce one big happy church that will usher in an era of peace and prosperity? Or are such practices the warning signs which indicate that God's judgment is near?

There are some evangelical Christians who are not the least bit concerned. "Don't worry, be happy," they say. For example, Charles and Frances Hunter, avid proponents of the "Holy Laughter" movement, declare:

> Let's follow God into the greatest and most powerful move ever seen in the history of the church! Listen and you'll hear a beautiful, heavenly sound coming down from the very

---

131. Sallie Cassidy, "Roman Catholics Experience Renewal," *Charisma*, July 1996, p. 18.

132. Ibid.

throne of Almighty God! It's not the sound of
God's anger! It's not the sound of God's wrath!
It's the sound of the joy of the Lord, the sound
of Holy Laughter![133]

133. Charles and Frances Hunter, *Holy Laughter*
    (Kingwood, TX: Hunter Books, 1994), p. 159.

15
Peace and Safety

Think about the scenario before us. Apostate Christians would rather "feel" or "experience" God than to trust and believe in His Word. Politically, economically, and religiously, the world has been prepared to accept a counterfeit Messiah, just as Bible prophecy foretold. Although the Bible warned that these things would precede the Second Coming of Jesus Christ, Christians and non-Christians have been blinded. Sometime soon the final curtain will be drawn. This present age will be over, and there will be no encore! Like the prophets of old, we have a message to proclaim. Are we willing to do our part and share the good news before it is too late?

HISTORY REPEATS ITSELF

The prophet Jeremiah was called by God to speak a tough message to the people of his day. They had turned away from the authority of the Word of God and had followed after the pagan practices of the surrounding nations. Under the inspiration of the Holy Spirit, Jeremiah pleaded with his generation. He stated:

> Thus saith the LORD of hosts, Hearken not unto the words of the prophets that prophesy unto you: they make you vain: they speak a vision of their own heart, and not out of the mouth of the LORD. They say still unto them that despise me, The LORD hath said, Ye shall have peace; and they say unto every one that walketh after the imagination of his own heart, No evil shall come upon you. For who hath stood in the counsel of the LORD, and hath perceived and heard his word? who hath marked his word, and heard it? Behold, a whirlwind of the LORD is gone forth in fury, even a grievous whirlwind: it shall fall grievously upon the head of the wicked. The anger of the LORD shall not return, until he have executed, and till he have performed the thoughts of his heart.[134]

This message of peace and safety that false prophets and teachers have proclaimed before the judgment of God has occurred is consistent with Satan's agenda throughout history. As Jeremiah continued in his heartfelt plea to his people:

> In the latter days ye shall consider it perfectly. I have not sent these prophets, yet they ran: I have not spoken to them, yet they prophesied. But if they had stood in my counsel, and had caused my people to hear my words, then they

---

134. Jeremiah 23:16–20.

should have turned them from their evil way, and from the evil of their doings. [135]

PAUL'S WARNING

The apostle Paul also warned the church about the last-days seduction that will occur in the name of peace. Although self-proclaimed prophets and Bible teachers are saying that we have "no worries" because apostasy is a thing of the past and that a "laughing revival" shows that God is blessing us, is this really true?

If laughing, shaking, jerking, deep breathing, and behaving like an animal are really gifts from God for the last-days church, then why didn't Jesus or any of the New Testament writers mention them? Such profound behavior would certainly have been mentioned at least once in the Scriptures. Also, when it comes to the prophets proclaiming "peace and safety," we are instructed to be very careful about this subject. As Paul wrote to the Thessalonians about the coming day of the Lord:

> But of the times and the seasons, brethren, ye have no need that I write unto you. For yourselves know perfectly that the day of the Lord so cometh as a thief in the night. For when they shall say, Peace and safety; then sudden destruction cometh upon them, as

---

135. Jeremiah 23:20–22.

travail upon a woman with child; and they
shall not escape.[136]

The day of the Lord that Paul was talking
about is related to the Second Coming of Jesus
Christ. It is obvious a delusion that "everything is
fine" will be followed by a time when God's
wrath will be poured out upon the earth.[137]

When prominent religious leaders who claim
to be Christian embrace the idea that peace can be
attained by joining together with pagans, the time
for His wrath to be poured out may be very soon.

SUMMIT IN ASSISI

In October of 1986 a "summit for peace" in the
Italian city of Assisi was attended by 160 leaders
representing twelve different major religions.
Invited there by Pope John Paul II, these religious
leaders enthusiastically prayed for peace according
to their own spiritual traditions. *Time* magazine
reported that:

> For several hours last week, an unprecedented
> event put together under [the Pope's] auspices
> dramatized one of the greatest of all aspirations.
> At his invitation, leaders from the religions of
> the earth gathered under glowering skies in the
> tranquil medieval town of Assisi and, with
> quiet dignity, uttered prayers for world peace.
> The throng included rabbis wearing yarmulkes

---

136. 1 Thessalonians 5:1–3.
137. Revelation 6:17.

and Sikhs in turbans, Muslims praying on thick carpets and a Zoroastrian kindling a fire.[138]

On this same occasion, Pope John Paul II allowed his good friend the Dalai Lama to replace the cross with a statue of Buddha on the altar of St. Peter's Church in Assisi so that he and his Buddhist monks could perform their worship there. As *Time* commented,

> The Pope's audience was aware that Assisi symbolically went well beyond the ceremonial friendship accorded other faiths by any previous Pontiff. The assemblage included not only monotheists but believers in creeds once labeled "heathen" and "pagan" by a church that for centuries had preached unambiguously that there was no salvation outside its walls.[139]

According to the *Time* article the spiritual summit went off without a hitch as the various religious representatives prayed according to their own customs:

> Difficulties that were expected to happen did not materialize. Hindus and Sikhs were assigned to the same church to offer their prayers, but did so with no friction. At another church, two Buddhists chanted and rhythmically beat thin drums. Outside on the grass, Shintoists played bamboo reed

---

138. *Time*, November 10, 1986, p. 78.
139. Ibid.

instruments. The result was more a spiritual harmony than a clashing dissonance. [140]

Time records several of the prayers for peace that were uttered by the religious representatives in Assisi. For example, while smoking a ceremonial peace pipe, John Pretty-on-Top, a Crow Indian medicine man from Montana in full-feathered headdress, recited: "O Great Spirit, I raise my pipe to you, to your messengers the four winds, and to mother earth, who provides for your children. I pray that you bring peace to all my brothers and sisters in this world."[141]

It is obvious that although this summit was arranged by the Catholic Pontiff in the name of Christianity, the theme of the conference was not Christian. The "worship" and the "prayers" that were offered at Assisi were an abomination to the God of the Bible. According to the Old Testament it is apparent that God hated and judged these same kinds of practices in the past.[142] Is there any reason to believe that God has changed?

A CUP OF TREMBLING

The prophet Zechariah prophesied that in the last days the city of Jerusalem would be recognized by the whole world as a major trouble spot. His proclamation, made by the inspiration of

---

140. Ibid., p. 79.
141. Ibid.
142. 2 Kings 17:9–18.

the Holy Spirit, is very relevant to the current events that are happening. He prophesied:

> The burden of the word of the LORD for Israel, saith the LORD, which stretcheth forth the heavens, and layeth the foundation of the earth, and formeth the spirit of man within him. Behold, I will make Jerusalem a cup of trembling unto all the people round about, when they shall be in the siege both against Judah and against Jerusalem. And in that day will I make Jerusalem a burdensome stone for all people: all that burden themselves with it shall be cut in pieces, though all the people of the earth be gathered together against it.[143]

Ever since Israel was reestablished as a nation after being in exile for almost 2,000 years, this tiny little country has been observed as one of the major trouble spots in the world. The bloody conflict between the Jews and the Muslims is constantly in the news. Although there have always been wars and rumors of wars throughout the world, the Middle East situation is unique. Everyone watches this region attentively—not just for political and economic reasons, but especially for the concern that there be a solution to bring about religious peace between Muslims and Jews.

Although summits, conferences, and treaties are implemented to seek the ultimate solution for a

---

143. Zechariah 12:1–3.

peace settlement, no one yet seems to have the answer.

A JOINT SOLUTION

A foundational premise of Judaism is that the Messiah will soon be coming and that the world will enter a period of peace known as the Messianic Age. Although Christians believe that the Messiah has already come in the person of Jesus Christ, they also believe that He will come again. While some Christians believe that the Kingdom of God can only be established when the Prince of Peace, Jesus Christ, literally returns, many professing Christians, including Catholics, believe that they will first establish the Kingdom themselves.

This "Kingdom Now" theology is also being embraced by many New Wine proponents and is becoming more widely accepted. Since preparing for the return of the Lord is central to this belief, the rebuilding of the Temple on the Holy Mount in Jerusalem is an important part of the plan to prepare for Jesus' return.

The Jews believe that the Messiah will set up His throne on the Holy Mount. In fact, at present a group called the Temple Institute located in the Jewish Quarters of the Old City of Jerusalem is committed to preparing the various elements that were used in the Temple in the past. They believe that the Temple will be built sometime soon in the future on the Holy Mount. They believe that though the Temple and the worship that will occur there will be based on Jewish traditions, the Temple will not be limited to Jews alone. The Temple will be a world center where all religions will be welcome to come and worship God in their own way.[144]

While in Jerusalem during the spring of 1996, I had the opportunity of visiting the Temple Institute. There I purchased a book called *Jerusalem, The Eye of the Universe*. Regarding Jerusalem being the religious focus of the world we read:

> Since this spot is where all spiritual forces come together to influence the physical world, this is indeed the "Gate of Heaven." It is from this spot —between the two Cherubim on the Ark— that prophecy emanates, and through which all prayers are channeled. This spot is the focus of all spiritual forces, and all communication that we have with these forces is through this location. It is thus thought that spiritual channels emanate from the Foundation Stone, bringing spiritual sustenance to all the world.[145]

---

144. "On the Altar," *Temple Institute Newsletter*, Volume 101, Summer 1996.
145. Aryeh Kaplan, *Jerusalem, The Eye of the Universe* (New York, NY: National Conference of Synagogue Youth, 1976), p. 82.

It is common knowledge that the Muslims also believe that the Holy Mount is one of the most sacred places on Earth. Although there is no proof, they believe this is where Mohammed was resurrected into heaven. The Muslims have religious authority over the Holy Mount and have built the Dome of the Rock and the Al-Aqsa mosque there for the worship of Allah.

How could this location, which is so sacred to the Muslims, become the site of a temple to serve as a center of ecumenical worship and peace?

Or what about a center of worship that would be implemented by a third, neutral religious group? After all, this same spot is sacred for Christians. What if a Christian leader proposed a solution? What about the head of the Catholic Church?

AN INTERNATIONAL CITY

The ethnic, political, and religious differences in the Middle-East have created a critical situation that has kept diplomats in turmoil. Since the "Declaration of Principles" was signed between Palestinian and Israeli leaders on the White House lawn on September 13, 1993, a major problem remains. If there is truly to be peace between Jews and Muslims, who would be in charge of the Old City of Jerusalem?

There are some people today who live in Jerusalem who say that they know how the peace of Jerusalem will be negotiated in the future. They say that the Old City of Jerusalem will eventually become an international city under the authority of the Vatican.

WHAT IF?

What if someday we open the morning paper and read the headlines: "Pope—New Mayor of Old Jerusalem." What would this mean? To the world, a "Christian" remedy to a Jewish-Muslim problem might sound like a perfect answer for peace. However, from a Bible prophecy perspective, if such a thing happened another key event would have been fulfilled. If a Christian leader like the pope declared a temple on Mount Moriah to be the religious capital of the world, the scenario would be fully in place. Are we being prepared for the very time in history when a man could proclaim to the world that he is God?

16

The Miracle Man

A form of Christianity based on all kinds of experiences that are not biblically based opens the door to spiritual deception. Although the God of the Bible is a God of miracles and performs signs and wonders according to His sovereign will, we must be very careful not to seek God based merely on miraculous signs. When people followed Jesus in order to seek after miracles, He distanced Himself from them, knowing that their faith was not based on a solid foundation.[146] Satan and his demonic hosts are fully capable of masquerading in the name of Christ by enticing people to believe because they have experienced the spiritual dimension in some way. However, saying that someone has become a Christian just because he or she has had a supernatural experience in Jesus' name may be the ultimate delusion.

---

146. John 2:23–25.

THE BLACK MADONNA

Signs and wonders in the name of Jesus are common occurrences. However, some of them are obviously extrabiblical in nature. How bizarre must miracles become before Christians will realize that not all supernatural activity is from God?

As one example of what some people call a "sign and wonder" we could quote a report from the "Charismatters" section of the March, 1996 issue of *Charisma* magazine. According to this article, thousands of people have been healed by walking past a portrait of a black Virgin Mary and infant Jesus that is hanging in a monastery in Poland.

The readers of this article are told that this is a miracle of God. Priests and nuns have reported that a woman was healed from multiple sclerosis, and others who were paralyzed or had terminal illnesses have been restored to full health. The article stated that even Pope John Paul II himself has visited the monastery to see the miracle-working Black Madonna and gave his blessing on the "miracles" that have been happening there.[147]

THIS IS THE ONE

Paul states that the man who will "sit in the temple of God, showing himself that he is God"[148]

---

147. *Charisma*, March 1996, p. 13.
148. 2 Thessalonians 2:4.

will be a miracle-worker. It is obvious that the source of his miracle-working power is not God, but Satan. Paul describes this clearly by stating:

> Even him, whose coming is after the working of Satan with all power and signs and lying wonders, and with all deceivableness of unrighteousness in them that perish; because they received not the love of the truth, that they might be saved. And for this cause God shall send them strong delusion, that they should believe a lie: that they all might be damned who believed not the truth, but had pleasure in unrighteousness.[149]

The Bible also teaches that this man who claims that he is the "king of kings" will rule and reign in conjunction with another religious leader who will endorse him. In line with the fact that the Jewish kings were always supported by a prophet of God, this self-proclaimed Jewish Messiah will do the same.

A FUTURE UNHOLY SPIRIT BARTENDER

It appears that even Bible-believing Christians are prepared to accept that a man can be a "Holy Spirit bartender" as part of the "new thing" that God is doing. If so, when delusion increases, could it not be possible for a form of Christianity to unite with other beliefs based on experiencing false signs and wonders?

---

149. 2 Thessalonians 2:9–12.

What if the false prophet were a well-known Christian leader who had already endorsed occultic practices in the name of Jesus Christ? What if he were to say that the Messiah had returned? What if the Jewish people were to accept this man as their Messiah? What if New Age supporters said "this is a man who has made the quantum leap of evolution"? Is the world being prepared?

Certainly these questions are only hypothetical. However, remember, if we are going to take the Bible seriously, we must recognize that the counterfeit bride for the counterfeit Christ will be an all-embracing form of Christianity based upon a reintroduction of ancient Babylonianism. This is why it is so imperative for Christians today to know who Jesus Christ is based on a knowledge of His Word. New Wine experiences may be real experiences, but what is their real source?

TOO DRUNK TO DRIVE

> My husband is not even saved, and he was more anxious to get to church than I was. But if he hasn't come to a decision for Christ yet, he's certainly on the brink. He came out of the meeting at Pensacola [Brownsville Assembly of God, Pensacola, Florida] so drunk in the Spirit

that he couldn't drive properly, and he went up
on the median divider.[150]

HE BELIEVED

A man came to our church because his sister
invited him. He was not a believer, so when
she told him what was happening, he said
"Yeah, right." He did not want to be rude so he
came with her. He became nervous when he
saw the dancing and laughing. Then someone
came up and asked if he wanted to be prayed
for. He said sure. Immediately he fell down. He
thought to himself, "That was really neat." He
got up and asked someone else to pray for him.
He fell down again and started tumbling
around in circles. "After that," he stated
emphatically, "I believed."[151]

HE NEVER KNEW THEM

Ever since the early church, the word
"Christian" has been used to describe a person
who is a follower of Jesus Christ. Although many
people claim they are "Christian," there are many
interpretations of what it actually means.

This book started with a discussion of what it
means to be a Christian from a biblical
perspective. Jesus said the way to eternal life is

---

150. awakening@pawn.spencer-davis.com. July 11,
    1996, subject, Brownsville Assembly of God.
151. John Arnott, *The Father's Blessing* (Orlando, FL:
    Creation House, 1995), first edition, p. 78.

narrow and that He is the only way. The gospel, the good news that transforms lives, can never be compromised. Where we spend eternity depends on whether or not we understand and accept the true gospel message. It is of infinite importance that we make the right decision.

The Scriptures also reveal the good news of salvation provided by Jesus Christ has always been, and will always be, opposed by Satan. Satan's methods to deceive are varied and diverse. Although one of his most successful techniques is to convince people to reject Jesus Christ, another one of his tactics is to deceive people into believing they have a relationship with Jesus when in reality they do not. As Jesus stated:

> Not everyone who says to me, "Lord, Lord," will enter the kingdom of heaven, but only he who does the will of my Father who is in heaven. Many will say to me on that day, "Lord, Lord, did we not prophesy in your name, and in your name drive out demons and perform many miracles?" Then I will tell them plainly, "I never knew you. Away from me, you evildoers!"[152]

Jesus said that on judgment day people will come before Him who have been fooled into believing they are Christians. These people have experienced supernatural experiences in the name of Christ, but they have never had a relationship

---

152. Matthew 7:21–23.

with Jesus Christ. How could these people have been so terribly deceived? Jesus answered this question in the next few verses that follow His terrible "judgment day" scenario which shows that sincere people can be deceived:

> Therefore whosoever heareth these sayings of mine, and doeth them, I will liken him unto a wise man, which built his house upon a rock: And the rain descended, and the floods came, and the winds blew, and beat upon that house; and it fell not: for it was founded upon a rock. And every one that heareth these sayings of mine, and doeth them not, shall be likened unto a foolish man, which built his house upon the sand: And the rain descended, and the floods came, and the winds blew, and beat upon that house; and it fell: and great was the fall of it.[153]

HAVE FAITH IN THE GOSPEL

There is only one gospel. Adding to the gospel or taking away from the gospel will produce "another gospel" which can send sincere people to hell.

Let us be like the Bereans who Luke commended for their earnest desire to check out all they were taught by the Scriptures.[154] To do anything less may well bring about spiritual suicide in these last important days of time.

---

153. Matthew 7:24–27.
154. Acts 17:11.

Epilogue

I charge thee therefore before God, and the Lord Jesus Christ, who shall judge the quick and the dead at his appearing and his kingdom;

Preach the word; be instant in season, out of season; reprove, rebuke, exhort with all longsuffering and doctrine.

For the time will come when they will not endure sound doctrine; but after their own lusts shall they heap to themselves teachers, having itching ears;

And they shall turn away their ears from the truth, and shall be turned to fables.

But watch thou in all things, endure afflictions, do the work of an evangelist, make full proof of thy ministry.

2 Timothy 4:1–5

More about the ministry of Understand The Times

Understand The Times is a nonprofit ministry founded by Roger Oakland. The ministry exists to give biblical insights for contemporary issues and to show how the Bible helps us understand the past, what is happening in the world today, and where we are headed in the future.

You can obtain a catalog of other books, cassettes and videos that have been developed to strengthen the faith of Christians and challenge unbelievers about what they believe by contacting the ministry offices in the following locations:

Understand The Times
P.O. Box 27239
Santa Ana, CA 92799 USA
1 (800) 689-1888

Understand The Times
P.O. Box 1160
Eston, Saskatchewan, Canada SOL 1AO

Understand The Times
Hall Street, New Stevenston
Motherwell, Scotland, United Kingdom ML 4LX

Visit the Understand The Times web site at:
http://www.understandthetimes.org